BROTHERS IN LAW

A Comedy in Three Acts

by

TED WILLIS and HENRY CECIL

Adapted from the book of the same name

by

HENRY CECIL

LONDON

SAMUEL FRENCH LIMITED

SAMUEL FRENCH LTD
26 SOUTHAMPTON STREET, STRAND, LONDON, W.C.2

SAMUEL FRENCH INC.
25 WEST 45TH STREET, NEW YORK, U.S.A.
7623 SUNSET BOULEVARD, HOLLYWOOD 46, CAL.

SAMUEL FRENCH (CANADA) LTD
27 GRENVILLE STREET, TORONTO

SAMUEL FRENCH (AUSTRALIA) PTY LTD
159 FORBES STREET, SYDNEY

MADE AND PRINTED IN GREAT BRITAIN BY
LATIMER, TREND AND CO., LTD, PLYMOUTH

MADE IN ENGLAND

822.91

BROTHERS IN LAW

First produced at the New Theatre, Bromley, in February 1957

CHARACTERS

(in the order of their appearance)

ALEC BLAKE, a barrister's clerk
SALLY MANNERING
MRS THURSBY, Roger's mother
ROGER THURSBY, a very young barrister
KENDALL GRIMES, a barrister
HENRY BLAGROVE, a barrister
MR GREEN, a client
MR BRADLEY, a young solicitor's clerk
JOY AMBLER
MR MERIVALE, a solicitor
MRS NEWENT, a client
MR JUSTICE KING, a judge
THE CLERK OF ASSIZE
AN USHER
A WARDER

SYNOPSIS OF SCENES

ACT I

SCENE 1   The Pupils' Room at Mr Grimes' chambers, Temple Court, London. Morning
SCENE 2   The same. A few days later. Morning

ACT II

The same. Wednesday, a few days later. Morning

ACT III

A courtroom and corridor at Bilborough Assizes. Ten days later
(During Act III the lights are lowered for a few moments to denote a slight passage of time)

Time—the present

Photograph by Kenneth Simmons

To face page 1 — *"Brothers In Law"*

ACT I

SCENE I

SCENE—*The Pupils' Room at Mr Grimes' chambers, Temple Court, London. Morning.*

Temple Court is old, uncomfortable and dusty, and the general décor of the room does not depart from tradition. But there is also a solidity, a certain dignity about the building which is impressive and one can feel this even in the Pupils' Room. Being the Pupils' Room, however, it is also the least secluded. The door to the entrance hall and front door is down L. A door to the Clerks' Room is down R, and a door up R, approached by three steps and a small balconied landing leads to Mr Grimes' room. There is a window in an alcove up LC. Desks, with revolving chairs are R and LC. Upright chairs stand L of the desk R, R of the desk LC and against the wall above the door down L. There is a bench under the window and a bookcase L. A pedestal with a vase and a threefold screen stand R and L of the alcove respectively. A cupboard is in a small alcove R. There is a telephone on the desk LC. A picture of Grimes, in uniform, hangs on the wall L.

When the CURTAIN *rises, the room is deserted. After a moment,* ALEC BLAKE *enters down* R. *He is in his late forties, an efficient, affable, warm-hearted man, with an ordinary voice—certainly not Cockney, and on the other hand, it is not particularly cultured and not spurious Oxford. He carries a ledger and a fee-book under one arm and a pile of law books under the other. He dumps the law books on the desk* R.

ALEC. Put 'em away yourself. (*He crosses to* C *and picks up two briefs from the floor*) Tut, tut! (*He looks at the names, blows the dust off the briefs and tosses them on to the desk* R. *He then crosses to the desk* LC, *sits at it, opens his ledger and fee-book and makes entries in them*) Let's see. Brown v. Simpson. Opinion, three five six. Conference, two seven.

(*The telephone rings*)

(*He takes no notice at first of the telephone. As it goes on ringing he looks at his watch, then at the telephone*) Ring away! Who do you think we are? Midwives? (*He resumes work*) Hobbs v. Bankhouse. Statement of Claim, four six six. Interrogatives, three five six. (*He looks at the telephone*) Try again in ten minutes. I'm busy.

(*The telephone stops ringing.*

SALLY MANNERING *enters down* L. *She is young, efficient and pretty. She is dressed in a dark suit and carries her handbag and newspaper*)

SALLY (*moving to* R *of the desk* LC) Hullo, Alec. You're early.
I didn't think I should find anyone here. (*She puts the paper on the
desk*)

ALEC (*quite pleasantly, but making his meaning clear*) Nor did I,
Miss Mannering. It's the only time of the day I can write up the
ledgers.

SALLY (*putting her bag in the desk drawer*) I'm sorry, Alec. Please
don't bother to move.

ALEC. Oh—this is your desk? Sorry. Give me another few
minutes. It's the only tidy one in chambers. Might have known.

SALLY. I promised to look up something for Mr Blagrove in the
Bar Library. He wants it for an early conference.

ALEC. I see. (*He resumes work*)

(SALLY *picks up a brief from the desk* LC, *moves* C, *opens the brief
and studies it*)

SALLY. Alec.

ALEC (*writing*) Opinion, two four six. Brief on summons, three
five six. Conference, two seven.

SALLY. I didn't mean to interrupt you. I'm sorry.

ALEC. Brief on hearing, twenty one fifteen—no, that's wrong.
(*To Sally*) What was it?

SALLY. Alec—tell me honestly—will I ever get any work at the
Bar?

ALEC. Oh, was that all? Just a moment. (*He looks at his figures*)
No, that can't be right. Oh, p'raps it is. (*To Sally, but without
looking up*) They all ask that. Your guess is as good as mine.

SALLY. But I'm a woman. It's so much more difficult.

ALEC. That's true. Three five six, seven twelve, fifteen ten—
then why don't you marry Mr Blagrove?

SALLY. I beg your pardon—what did you say?

ALEC. Drafting statement of claim, four six six; drafting reply,
three six six. (*He looks up*) I'm sure he's asked you.

SALLY. Even if he has, that's no answer to my question.

ALEC. It's the only one I can think of at the moment. As you
said—it's difficult for a woman.

SALLY (*crossing to the door down* L; *slightly annoyed*) I'm going to
the library.

ALEC. Don't shut the outer door, please. I'm expecting someone.

SALLY. O.K. Thank you for being so helpful!

(SALLY *snorts and exits down* L. ALEC *sighs and looks at his watch.
The telephone rings*)

ALEC. Oh, well.

(ALEC *rises, picks up his ledger and fee-book, crosses and exits down*
R. *The telephone continues to ring. There is a gentle knock on the door
down* L.)

*Mrs Thursby and Roger Thursby enter down l. Mrs
Thursby is a young forty-eight, well-dressed, attractive and kind.
She is constitutionally incapable of concentrating on any one line of
conversation for very long. Roger is aged twenty-four and is understandably nervous, for he has just been called, and has had no experience of
the practical side of the law. He is carrying a barrister's blue bag containing his robes. He is not at all sure whether they should enter like
this and dithers in the doorway. He transfers the bag from one hand to
the other for quite a time, as though he is not sure of staying*

Roger. Shouldn't we have rung?

Mrs Thursby (*moving below the desk* LC) I don't think they'd
have heard us. (*She reaches out to answer the telephone*)

(*The telephone ringing stops abruptly*)

Oh!

Roger. Oughtn't we to wait outside, Mother?

Mrs Thursby (*crossing to the desk* R) Mr Grimes won't mind. I
told you, we're *old* friends—well, friends, anyway. It's just that
we've lost touch the last few years.

Roger (*crossing to* C) Bit of luck for me. He's one of the busiest
juniors at the Bar.

Mrs Thursby. Well, I'm sure you'll be just as busy very soon.
It's simply a question of getting started. (*She displays her frock*)
You're sure you like this dress?

Roger (*turning to the desk* LC) Perfect. (*He picks up a pile of
briefs from the desk*) Look at all these briefs. And I'd sell my soul
for just one.

Mrs Thursby. You mustn't expect too much in the first week.
But after that—well . . . (*Pensively*) Do you like the way this skirt
hangs? I mean—the way it seems to come from nowhere?

Roger. You look lovely. (*He replaces the briefs on the desk*)

Mrs Thursby. What did you say, dear?

Roger (*turning*) You look lovely.

Mrs Thursby (*going up the steps to the landing up* R) That's what
I thought you said. (*She turns and surveys the office*) I just wanted to
hear it again. Roger—would it help if we put a little notice in
The Times?

Roger. About what?

Mrs Thursby. About . . . Oh, look—(*she indicates the picture of
Grimes on the wall* L) there's a picture of Mr Grimes when he was
a soldier. He had a beautiful moustache in those days. (*She stands
admiring the picture*)

Roger. What were you saying about *The Times?*

Mrs Thursby. I wonder if it would help you to have a moustache? You look so young, you know. No—I think you should
try to succeed without one.

Roger. Thank you. *The Times*, Mother.

Mrs Thursby (*moving to the desk* R) *The Times?* Oh, yes—*The Times*. (*She puts her handbag on the desk*) Well, I was thinking—a discreet little notice in the Personal Column. Something simple —like—like—"Mr Roger Thursby, only son of Mrs Amanda Thursby and the late Colonel Thursby, wishes to announce that he has been called to the Bar and is now in practice in the Chambers of Mr Kendall Grimes. If you are in trouble, ring . . ." What's this number?

Roger. Barristers are not allowed to advertise.

Mrs Thursby. *The Times* isn't advertising, surely. (*She crosses to* L *of Roger*) No? Ah, well, I expect you'll manage without it— (*she chucks Roger under his chin*) just the same. (*She moves to the desk* LC)

Roger. I wish I had your confidence.

Mrs Thursby (*smelling the flowers on the desk* LC; *seriously*) It never enters my head that you won't succeed, you know, because —well, it never enters my head.

Roger. I couldn't have got through this far without you.

Mrs Thursby. Oh, nonsense! I haven't the brains of a butterfly. (*She crosses to* RC) You know, I can't wait for the time when you'll come home with one of those bags bulging with briefs— (*she pauses suddenly*) I suppose that must be why they call them "brief-cases"—I never realized—and you tell me all the details of your latest divorce.

Roger (*with the slight pomposity of the beginner*) A barrister is not allowed to discuss his clients with outsiders.

Mrs Thursby. Well, I'm not an outsider. Can't you trust me?

Roger (*smiling*) No.

Mrs Thursby. Roger—that hurts. I wouldn't discuss your cases with anyone—except perhaps just a few close personal friends.

Roger (*smiling*) You know, there's no-one like you. I swear it. No-one in the whole world.

Mrs Thursby (*pleased*) Perhaps you're right—I suppose I do let my tongue run away with me sometimes. I can't help it. I like talking. (*She looks at the portrait*) Dear Kennie—I wonder if he's altered very much.

(Alec *enters down* R. *He carries a file of papers*)

Alec. Good morning, Mrs Thursby.

Mrs Thursby. Oh—good morning. Mr Blake, isn't it?

Alec. That's it. (*He crosses to Roger*) That would be young Mr Thursby, eh? (*He shakes hands with Roger*) Pleased to meet you, sir.

Mrs Thursby. I hope it's all right my bringing Roger. I wanted to see Kennie—Mr Grimes, to see if he can take Roger as a pupil or whatever it is you call them.

Alec. Yes, Mrs Thursby. Mr Grimes knows about it.

Mrs Thursby. He will be able to—won't he?
Alec. Ah, that's for Mr Grimes to say.

(Roger *moves down* l *of the desk* lc)

(*He points to Roger's bag*) But I see you've come prepared.
Mrs Thursby. Ah, the robes. He looks wonderful in them. And the wig . . .
Alec. They do add something, don't they? Now, if you'll excuse me, I must start Mr Grimes' telephone calls. He'll take them in here today—his phone's out of order. (*He crosses to the door down* r) Do sit down, Mrs Thursby.

(Alec *exits down* r. *There is a slight pause, then there is a noise on the stairs off* l *rather like a small express train.*
     Kendall Grimes *rushes in down* l. Roger *is rather in his way.* Grimes *eventually gets past Roger, hands him his hat, goes to the telephone and lifts the receiver*)

Mrs Thursby. Kennie! (*She crosses to* r *of Grimes*)

(Grimes *is at first too busy at the telephone to notice Mrs Thursby*)

Grimes (*into the telephone*) Hullo, hullo—Alec, get me Mr Grey . . . Oh, you're there—how are you, my dear fellow? . . . That's quite all right . . . Now, don't ye worry, m'dear fellow, just go to the Master and tell him the tale, tell him the tale . . . Good, good—thank ye so much . . . Bye, bye. (*He clicks the receiver rest*) Hello . . . Ah, Mr Arkwright . . . How are ye? . . . Mmmm? . . . Well as can be expected m'dear fellow . . . What's that? . . . Well, well, well—they will do these things, y'know—the fellers will be fellers and the girls will be girls . . . Yes, of course we'll put in a defence . . . About two-thirty? . . . Excellent, my dear fellow, I'll be waiting. (*He clicks the receiver rest*) Copley? . . . My dear fellow, how are ye? . . . Now, Copley, m'dear chap, about your little business. Just issue a summons, just issue a summons . . . Mmm? . . . Ah, the Judge in Chambers will have something to say about that . . . (*He suddenly becomes aware of Mrs Thursby standing near him, smiling. At first he smiles back and listens to the telephone, then, as the penny drops, he puts the receiver on the desk and advances on Mrs Thursby with outstretched hands*) Amanda! Amanda—my dear girl, how are you?
Mrs Thursby. Kennie . . .

(Roger *moves to* l *of Grimes, hoping to be recognized*)

Grimes (*to Roger*) Just tell him to hold on, m'dear fellow.
Roger. Eh? Oh—yes. (*He puts the hat on the desk and picks up the receiver. Into the telephone*) Hullo . . . Oh . . . Could you hold the line, please . . .
Grimes. Amanda. It must be—oh, how many years since . . .

Mrs Thursby. Don't remind me, Kennie. You haven't changed.

Grimes. Oh—I'm not so sure. Can't get around like I used to, you know. You're as beautiful as ever.

Roger (*to Grimes*) Excuse me, sir . . .

Grimes. Just tell him the tale, m'dear fellow, tell him the tale.

Roger (*into the telephone*) Mr Grimes won't be long . . . I beg your pardon? . . . Well—he's—he's looking at an old brief . . .

(Grimes *and* Mrs Thursby *turn and stare at* Roger *who claps his hand over his mouth in embarrassment*)

Grimes (*to Mrs Thursby*) Remember our picnics?

Mrs Thursby. Oh, yes—the picnics—down the Thames.

Grimes. Or it may have been up. I can never remember. But they were wonderful. Well, well, well—fancy seeing you again. Sit down, m'dear.

(Mrs Thursby *sits on the chair* L *of the desk* R. Roger *replaces the receiver*)

Roger. Excuse me . . .

Grimes. What is it now?

Roger. He's hung up.

Grimes. Good. Just tell him I'll ring back in five minutes.

(Roger *nods brightly, lifts the receiver, realizes it is useless and replaces it*)

(*He crosses and leans on the desk* R) Well—well—well. Amanda! You know, we must have dinner—lunch—what are you doing for lunch today? No time like the present, y'know—the past's the past and we won't get very far just talking about that.

Mrs Thursby. I'd love to, Kennie. But we should really discuss Roger, shouldn't we?

(Roger *transfers his bag to his other hand*)

Roger—come here now. Over here. Kennie—this is Roger, my Roger.

(Roger *moves* C)

Grimes (*crossing to* R *of Roger*) How do ye do, young man?

Roger (*eagerly*) Very well, thank you, sir. I've heard an awful lot about you from mother.

Grimes. Ye have, have ye? Did she tell you about the picnics?

Mrs Thursby. Kennie . . .

Grimes. No, don't suppose ye did. I expect he has enough picnics of his own, eh? They will do these things, they will do these things. Well, what can we do for him, eh? Trouble of some kind?

Roger. Oh, no, sir . . .

GRIMES. Good, good—like to see young fellers keeping out of trouble. (*He turns to Mrs Thursby in whom he is chiefly interested*) Can't get over you, m'dear—known you anywhere—you're positively devastating, you know that?

MRS THURSBY. Kennie! We're here to talk about Roger.

GRIMES. Roger—ah, Roger. By all means. What are ye going in for, my boy?

ROGER. Well, actually . . .

GRIMES. Steer clear of the Law—wouldn't advise it. (*He calls*) Alec.

(ALEC *enters down* R)

Did Brookes telephone?

ALEC. No.

GRIMES. Get on to him at once, my dear fellow. And look after young Mr Trueband, here—I want to talk to his mother. (*He moves to the steps up* RC) This way, Amanda.

(MRS THURSBY *rises, picks up her handbag and goes up the steps*)

ROGER. But, sir—Mother . . .

(GRIMES *ushers* MRS THURSBY *off up* R. ROGER *is left with Alec*)

ALEC (*crossing to* R *of Roger*) You might as well put that bag down, sir—he'll probably be some time.

ROGER (*putting the bag on the floor* C) He called me "Trueband". Didn't even remember why I'd come.

ALEC. Don't worry, sir. Judges called *him* all sorts of names when he began. It'll be all right, sir. (*He takes a bag of toffees from his pocket*)

ROGER. Thank you.

ALEC (*offering the bag*) Have a toffee?

ROGER. No, thanks.

ALEC. Go on, sir—be a devil.

(ROGER *takes a toffee*)

That's the ticket. Now, if you'll excuse me—one or two little things to attend to.

(ALEC *crosses and exits down* L. ROGER *kicks his bag, removes the paper from the toffee, puts the toffee in his mouth and has difficulty with the paper. It is sticking to his fingers, and as he pulls it from one hand it fastens on to the fingers of the other.*
    SALLY *enters down* L)

SALLY (*curiously*) Good morning.

ROGER. Good morning.

(SALLY *removes her hat and coat, hangs them on the hooks up* L,

crosses to the desk R, *picks up the typewriter and transfers it to the desk*
LC)

ROGER (*following Sally*) Oh—let me help . . .
SALLY. Thank you. (*She smiles*) Done now.

(ROGER *steps back shyly, and almost trips over his bag*)

(*She sits at the desk* LC) Are you waiting to see Mr Grimes? (*She
puts a clean sheet of paper into the typewriter*)
ROGER. Yes.
SALLY (*banging away at the typewriter*) I don't suppose he will
keep you long. Won't you sit down?
ROGER. Thank you. (*He sits on the chair* L *of the desk* R)

(*There is a short pause as* SALLY *types*)

(*Chattily*) I expect they keep you pretty busy.
SALLY. Oh, yes.
ROGER. I mean—there must be an awful lot of typing in an
office like this.
SALLY (*slightly puzzled*) Quite a lot.
ROGER. I suppose there are other typists?

(SALLY *stops typing*)

I mean—they don't expect you to do it all, do they?
SALLY (*with a slight edge to her voice*) Oh, yes—there are others.
I'm not very good at it, you see. (*She demonstrates*) One finger—
one thumb.
ROGER. Ah, well—it's not the most important thing. I expect
you're very quick at shorthand.
SALLY. No, I'm not. If anything, that's worse than my typing.
ROGER (*a little taken aback*) Oh. (*He rises and crosses to Sally. Un-
defeated*) Well, when I dictate to you, I'll remember to take it
very, very slowly.
SALLY. Thank you. Thank you, Mr—er . . .
ROGER. Thursby. I'm coming into these chambers, y'know—
at least—I think I am—I'm a barrister, you know.
SALLY. Really? Since when, Mr Thursby?
ROGER (*awkwardly*) Well, actually . . .
SALLY. Yes?
ROGER. I was called—a short time ago.
SALLY. A short time?
ROGER. Actually . . .

(*The telephone rings.* SALLY, *with a glance at Roger, lifts the
receiver*)

SALLY (*into the telephone*) Miss Mannering here . . . Oh, yes,
Mr Bigley . . . A conference? . . . (*She makes notes*) Let me see . . .
How about next Monday—earlyish—say ten a.m.? . . . Yes . . .

Of course . . . Good-bye. (*She replaces the receiver, rises and crosses to the desk* R) You were saying, Mr Thursby?

ROGER (*hastily*) What is Mr Grimes like—to work for, I mean?

SALLY. He's terribly overworked. But now you've come, I'm sure things will be so much easier for him.

ROGER (*crossing to* L *of the desk*) Oh, I wouldn't say that. I mean —candidly—I've an awful lot to learn, you know.

SALLY. That's very hard to believe.

ROGER (*earnestly*) Honestly—I've no illusions—I've got to face up to things.

(HENRY BLAGROVE *enters briskly down* R. *He is aged about thirty and is lively, energetic and unconventional. He does not notice Roger*)

HENRY (*crossing to Sally*) 'Morning, Sally. Haven't seen you for twelve hours. (*He kisses her*)

SALLY (*for Roger's benefit*) Really, Mr Blagrove—in office hours.

(HENRY *notices* ROGER *who smiles at him rather nervously*)

HENRY (*to Roger*) 'Morning.

(ROGER *closes the door*)

SALLY. This is Mr Thursby. He may be coming here as a pupil.

(ROGER *crosses to* C)

HENRY. Another lamb for the pot, eh? Blagrove's my name. (*He shakes Roger's hand vigorously*) Expect you saw it on the door. Been here seven years myself. I started as a lamb—black sheep, now. Only thing that keeps me here is Sally.

SALLY (*crossing above the others to the desk* LC) Mr Thursby is a barrister. (*She sits at the desk*)

HENRY. Well, I didn't imagine he was a dustman, dear girl. You're moving in, are you, old boy?

ROGER. It's not absolutely settled, Mr Blagrove.

HENRY. No, no, no, no! "Blagrove", not "Mr Blagrove". Once you're called you refer to everyone at the Bar by his surname.

ROGER. Really? I mean—Q.C.s?

HENRY. Q.C.s—everyone.

ROGER. Even a judge?

HENRY. No. Judges are different. You just call them "Judge". If you ever run over a judge in your car, you just pick him up, dust him down, and say: "Sorry, Judge", or "You ought to be more careful, Judge".

SALLY. Anyway, it's going to be a lot easier for you and Grimey—I mean Mr Grimes—when Mr Thursby joins us.

ROGER. Well, as I was just saying—I've had no practical experience really . . .

HENRY (*sitting at the desk* R) Practical experience? That's a greatly overrated commodity, old chap. The Divorce Courts are jammed with people who have had bags of practical experience— but ninety per cent of 'em go and make the same mistake again.

ROGER. I see what you mean. I was thinking of experience in the practice of law. (*He moves above the desk* R)

HENRY. Ignore me, m'dear chap. I'm the facetious type. I'll never make the grade.

(MRS THURSBY *enters up* R)

MRS THURSBY (*tapping Roger's head over the rail*) Roger, dear— come and talk to Mr Grimes.

ROGER. Oh—yes—coming. (*To the others*) Excuse me. (*He turns to the steps, remembers his bag and, smiling nervously, picks it up*)

(MRS THURSBY *exits up* R.
    ROGER *follows her off, closing the door behind him*)

HENRY (*rising*) Poor feller. (*He picks up a brief from the desk and crosses to Sally*) Reminds me of *my* first day. (*He puts the brief on the desk* LC) Who's the lady?

SALLY. That's mummy, I expect. What a specimen! The young man, I mean. You know, he thought I was a typist. If he comes here, I shall seriously consider moving . . .

HENRY. Where shall we go?

SALLY. Go away, Henry. I'm busy. I've wasted enough time already.

HENRY. All I want is a little encouragement.

SALLY. To work?

HENRY. Why not? But I need someone to work for. You, for instance.

SALLY. No, thank you.

HENRY. Don't be so definite. You haven't heard all the evidence. "My Lord, Blagrove would make a wonderful husband, and this young lady could continue her career at the Bar.

SALLY. And the children?

HENRY. So you have been thinking about it.

SALLY (*rising*) I have not. (*To cover her embarrassment she gets a book from the shelves* L)

HENRY. You mentioned the children. I see four—three girls and a boy. Only one boy because they're more expensive to educate.

SALLY (*resuming her seat*) Why should they be? The girls will get the same chance as the boys.

HENRY. Sally, darling . . .

SALLY. I mean—in a manner of speaking. Now, go away.

HENRY (*seriously and sincerely*) I'm not kidding, Sally. I'd work like a dog if you just raised your eyebrow.

SALLY. Henry—dear—you mustn't keep saying things like that.

HENRY. Why?

SALLY. It worries me—a little, anyway.

HENRY. Good! (*He bends over her*) Then I shall keep on saying them.

SALLY (*glancing towards the door up* R) Look out.

(MRS THURSBY, GRIMES *and* ROGER *enter up* R. ROGER *carries his bag.* HENRY *straightens up quickly.* SALLY *fiddles with her papers*)

GRIMES (*crossing to* C) Then that's all settled, eh?

(SALLY *and* HENRY *exchange glances*)

Don't blame me if it doesn't work out, Amanda. They will do these things.

MRS THURSBY (*crossing to* L *of Grimes*) But you will look after him, Kennie.

GRIMES. Ah, he'll have to take his chance—bit of a rough-and-tumble this life, m'dear boy—I hope you're ready for it.

ROGER (*moving above the desk* R) Of course, sir—of course.

GRIMES. Don't call me "sir", m'dear fellow. We're all equal here.

(HENRY *and* SALLY *again exchange glances*)

Now, tell me, m'dear fellow, have you the speed of a greyhound, the strength of an ox and the memory of an elephant? Have you, m'dear Trueband?

ROGER. Well—er . . .

GRIMES. You have, m'dear fellow? Then when would you like to start?

ROGER. At once, if I may.

GRIMES (*crossing and picking up some briefs from the desk* R) Then take these and have a look at them. (*He thrusts the briefs into Roger's hand*) Find yourself a desk here—this is the pupils' room. (*He turns to Mrs Thursby*) See you at lunch, Amanda. (*He leads Mrs Thursby to the door down* L) Twelve-forty-five—good.

MRS THURSBY. Thank you, Kennie. I'm sure you won't regret it. He's terribly clever.

ROGER. Mother!

MRS THURSBY. He hates praise. But it's perfectly true. Twelve-forty-five, then. 'Bye. Be good now, Roger.

(MRS THURSBY *waves to Roger, smiles at Sally, throws a kiss to Grimes and exits down* L. GRIMES *looks thoughtfully after her for a moment and smiles reflectively*)

GRIMES (*to himself*) Well, well, well. Picnics, cucumber sandwiches—we would do these things, we would do 'em. (*He crosses to the steps. To Roger*) Anything you want, m'dear fellow—just ask. What's your name?

ROGER. "Thursby—Roger Thursby."

GRIMES. "Thursby", eh? I thought someone said it was "True-band".

(GRIMES *exits up* R. ROGER *looks at the briefs, then at Henry and Sally. He still holds his bag*)

HENRY (*crossing to* L *of Roger*) Welcome to the stable, old boy. (*He takes the bag from Roger and puts it on the floor up* C) Here, you can have this desk.

ROGER. Thank you. (*He sits rather nervously at the desk* R)

HENRY (*sitting on the upstage end of the desk*) That's it. You look the part now. What's old Grimey-boy given you? (*He looks at the brief*) Ah, the good old Drum Bottling Company. I feel rather sentimental about that case—cut my teeth on it seven years ago.

ROGER. You mean it's still going on?

HENRY. Of course. No sense in rushing things. You'll soon get the hang of it all.

(ALEC *rushes in down* L. HENRY *rises*)

ALEC. Q.B. Court six first, then the Official Referee. (*He turns to rush out*)

HENRY (*checking Alec*) Alec—Mr Thursby is joining us.

ALEC. Oh—pleased to have you, sir. You've met everyone—Mr Blagrove—and Miss Mannering, your fellow pupil.

ROGER (*rising*) Fellow pupil?

HENRY. That's right, old boy. Three months to go.

ALEC. Come along to court, sir, in half a minute.

(ALEC *rushes out down* L)

ROGER (*crossing to Sally; really embarrassed*) Oh, I say—Miss Mannering—I really am most frightfully sorry . . .

SALLY (*coldly*) That's all right. (*She rises*)

HENRY. Recommended to mercy on account of his youth.

ROGER. I mean—you see—when you lifted the typewriter—I didn't realize . . .

HENRY. Of course he didn't. And I bet you were stringing him along.

SALLY (*smiling*) It's all right. (*She shakes Roger's hand*) You're discharged. It was partly my fault.

(GRIMES *rushes in up* R, *carrying his wig and putting on his gown and bands*)

GRIMES. Come on, m'dear feller. Plenty of time for introductions later—come and see what it's all about.

(GRIMES *exits down* L)

SALLY (*moving down* L) We're off. (*To Roger*) Come on—we're in this procession.

HENRY. Now you'll see what he meant by the speed of a grey-hound. He'll be half-way down the Strand by now.
SALLY. Come on.

(SALLY *and* ROGER *rush out down* L. HENRY *picks up Roger's bag*)

HENRY (*calling*) Hey!

(ROGER *re-enters down* L)

ROGER. Yes?
HENRY. Your robes. You'll need them. (*He tosses the bag to Roger*)
ROGER (*catching the bag*) Thanks.
SALLY (*off; calling*) Come on.
ROGER (*to Henry*) I say—what do I call *her?*
HENRY. What? Oh, I see. Well, I call her "darling".
ROGER (*seriously*) Oh. (*He turns and calls*) Hey, wait for me, darling.

ROGER *rushes off down* L *as—*

the CURTAIN *falls*

SCENE 2

SCENE—*The same. A few days later. Morning.*

When the CURTAIN *rises,* SALLY *is seated at the desk* LC *and* ROGER *is seated at the desk* R. *Both are studying documents.*

ROGER (*after a pause*) Oh, no! (*He rises*)
SALLY (*looking up*) I beg your pardon.
ROGER (*crossing to* R *of Sally*) Really! "My dearest, sweetest turnip . . ."
SALLY. What's that?
ROGER. I was just quoting—from these letters. "Dearest, sweetest turnip"—did you ever hear anything so revolting?
SALLY. What's the case? (*She looks at Roger's documents*) Oh, Biggs and Pieman. That's nothing.
ROGER. Listen—this is the end of the first letter she wrote him. (*He reads*) "My own sweet darling, my turnip—I adore you."
SALLY. Mmm—sounds just like the end of the first letter. They're always like that. Now try the last letter.
ROGER (*looking through the documents*) The last one? (*He moves* C)
SALLY. How does that finish?
ROGER (*reading*) "Dear Mr Pieman, If I do not receive your cheque by return, I shall have no alternative but legal action."

B

SALLY (*rising*) From "my darling turnip" to "legal action" in six months. That's life.

ROGER. I think it's horrible! I'm sure that if I fell in love . . .

SALLY. Yes? (*She glances towards the door up* R *and resumes her seat*)

(GRIMES *bustles in up* R *carrying a brief*)

GRIMES (*crossing to Sally*) Just have a look at this Opinion for me, will ye, my dear girl? (*He drops the brief on the desk*) See if I've made any mistakes. (*He turns to Roger*) How are ye? Hard at it, eh? (*He looks at Roger's documents*) What's this? Ah—our friend Pieman—shouldn't worry too much about that. It'll never come to court—neither of them want the publicity.

ROGER. Mother knows a Mrs Biggs. I wonder if it's the same.

GRIMES (*leading Roger down* C) Don't ask her, my boy. That's something you must remember. Anything you read or hear of in these chambers—strictly confidential. Not a word to a soul. If people knew what we've got in some of these papers . . . Mmm—not a word, m'dear fellow.

ROGER. Oh, I wouldn't dream of it.

GRIMES. Good—good. They will do these things, you know, they will do these things. But they shouldn't. Well—not as often as they do. Should they, m'dear fellow?

ROGER. I—er—suppose not.

GRIMES (*briskly*) Y'don't know what I'm talking about, m'dear fellow, do you?

ROGER. Er—no.

GRIMES. Then you've a chance of getting on. Never pretend to understand when ye don't.

SALLY. Mr Grimes, I've been going into Fisher and Millett. (*She rises, picks up her documents, moves below the desk* LC *and leans on it*) Are they still fighting the trousers?

GRIMES. Oh, yes. (*To Roger*) Listen to this, my boy. It's typical. A running-down case.

ROGER (*eager*) A car accident?

GRIMES. That's it. The defendant admits the damage to the car, but for some reason he's fighting the trousers.

ROGER. Fighting the trousers?

GRIMES (*sitting on the chair* R *of the desk* LC) Won't pay for them. Can't think why not. Does he think she don't wear trousers?

SALLY. I was found in the sump after the accident, so it can't have done the trousers any good, can it?

GRIMES. They were ruined.

SALLY. They had to be cut off me.

ROGER. You were involved?

SALLY. Of course not. (*To Grimes*) I kept the pieces. But I can't remember where I bought them.

Grimes. Ye'll have to try. Little things like trousers can make a lot of difference. If the judge doesn't believe the trousers he may not believe the accident.

Sally. But I was in hospital for three months.

Roger. You said you weren't involved.

Sally. I'm the client—not me.

Roger. Oh . . .

Sally. It's just the way we talk about cases—you'll soon get used to it.

Grimes. Like that business of the bananas that went bad. Ye would say—"I am the owner of a lot of rotten bananas", but ye wouldn't be. D'ye see, my dear fellow?

Roger (*doubtfully*) Yes . . .

Sally. You just put yourself in the place of your client. (*To Grimes*) The defendants don't believe the trousers were cut off me after the accident.

Grimes. What do they say?

Sally. They think I took them off in the ordinary way.

Grimes. Ah, ah—do you remember when ye last took them off before the accident? Did anyone see ye?

Sally (*after a quick glance at the documents*) Yes—we went bathing.

Grimes. Had ye a bathing costume?

Sally. No. There were only men around, so I didn't bother . . .

Grimes. There are your witnesses. Ye can call them to say ye put the trousers on again.

Sally. I didn't know them. They were just some chaps I met in a pub.

Roger. Look, I don't quite . . . Oh, of course—like rotten bananas . . . (*He moves* RC)

Grimes (*rising*) Exactly. Get down to it again, my dear girl, will ye? We'll show them who was wearing the trousers, won't we?

(Sally *moves and sits at the desk* LC.
Alec *puts his head round the door down* L)

Alec. Ah, there you are, sir. Mr Green is here to see you.

Grimes. Send him in, Alec. He can come this way.

(Alec *withdraws*)

(*He crosses to Roger*) Dare say you're finding all this very confusing—but ye'll get the hang of it in time. Just keep on asking questions—only way to learn, m'dear fellow. No good having a nice white wig if there's nothing under it, eh?

(Alec *enters down* L *and stands aside*)

Alec. Mr Green, sir.

(MR GREEN *enters down* L. *He is a cheeky, colourful Cockney, immensely sure of himself*)

GREEN (*crossing to* C) 'Morning, all—morning. How are we all today?

GRIMES (*crossing to* R *of Green*) How are ye, Mr Green, how are ye?

GREEN. You haven't changed much in twenty years, guv'nor. Come on a bit, I dare say—but who hasn't? I've jumped a bit myself—none of the old dock brief lark now—got meself a real live solicitor now. (*He looks towards the door down* L *and calls*) Oi, oi!

(MR BRADLEY *enters down* L *and crosses to* L *of Green.* BRADLEY *is a diminutive solicitor's clerk, aged fifteen*)

GRIMES. Capital, capital!

GREEN. Here, have a butcher's . . . (*He spins Bradley around*) Couldn't have afforded him twenty years back. Let me present Spindle, Hugg and Teeming, Solicitors and Commissioners for Oaths.

BRADLEY. Pleased to meet you, sir.

GREEN (*with pride*) Talks, too, you see. (*To Bradley*) Sit down, lad.

(BRADLEY *sits* R *of the desk* LC)

GRIMES (*dryly*) And which partner is this? Mr Spindle, Mr Hugg or Mr Teeming?

GREEN. This is Mr Bradley. He represents the firm. Ah, I know the rules, you see. Can't see counsel without someone from the solicitors there to see fair play.

GRIMES. And no-one else was available?

GREEN. You hit it, guv'nor. Mr Spindle—dead; Mr Hugg—dead; Mr Teeming—on his last legs; clerks run off their feet—not available. So they sent Mr Bradley. Nothing wrong with that, is there?

GRIMES. All in order, Mr Green. (*He moves up* R) Come into my room, will you?

GREEN (*indicating Roger and Sally*) This your stable?

GRIMES (*on the stairs*) These are my pupils, m'dear fellow—Miss Mannering and Mr Thursby—Mr Green.

GREEN. Pleased to meet you. (*Confidentially*) Let me give you a tip. I been in and out of more courts than you've had hot dinners. Look before you leap. Then close both eyes and jump.

SALLY. Thank you.

ROGER. Thank you.

GREEN. Any time. Well, let's get on with it, guv'nor. (*He moves up* R) I've got a little surprise for you, Mr Grimes. I'm innocent this time. Not guilty. It's old age, I suppose. Must be slipping. (*To Bradley*) Oi, come on, Sir Hartley.

(GRIMES *and* GREEN *exit up* R.

BRADLEY *rises and follows them off, closing the door behind them.* SALLY *laughs*)

ROGER (*moving* C; *rather in awe*) Is he a criminal?

SALLY. No-one is a criminal when they come here. They are all innocent—all we have to do is stop the prosecution proving they're not.

ROGER. I'll never learn it all. I mean—there's so much, um—er—er . . .

SALLY. Do you have to say "Um—er—er" whenever you speak to me? I have a name, you know.

ROGER. It's dashed awkward, you see. Henry told me that one always addressed a colleague by his surname—but I can't bring myself to call you "Mannering"—I mean—"Mannering"!

SALLY (*rising*) Call me "Sally" and I'll call you "Roger". That make it easier?

ROGER. Oh, much. (*He moves to* R *of Sally*) Um—er—er—I mean—Sally—are you busy tonight?

SALLY. Why?

ROGER. I thought we might have some dinner together.

SALLY. Why?

ROGER. Does there have to be a reason?

SALLY. Can't you think of one?

ROGER. Well, it would be nice. And I've got to eat—I mean—and I've a hundred questions to ask you about the chambers—and—it would be nice . . .

SALLY. You mean a business dinner?

ROGER. Yes—I mean, no, not exactly. But if you wouldn't mind—it would help an awful lot.

SALLY. I'll consider it. Henry has already asked me. I gave him the same answer.

ROGER. Oh—Henry . . .

SALLY. I like Henry.

ROGER. Oh, so do I. I like everyone here. Grimes, Henry, Alec, you . . .

SALLY (*sitting at the desk* LC) Thank you, Roger.

ROGER (*eagerly*) Oh, I mean it—absolutely. I think you're wonderful—I mean . . .

SALLY (*gently*) You'd better get on with Biggs and Pieman, don't you think?

ROGER (*moving* C) Biggs and Pieman. (*Reflectively*) I am a bedroom door. Mr Pieman says I was locked on the night in question. But was the key on my outside or inside? How's that?

SALLY. Excellent. You're learning fast.

ROGER (*ruefully*) I'm not. But I've got to. I've got to start earning some money. We're hard up, you know. If only there'd be a knock at that door and Alec walked through with a brief. For me!

(*There is a sudden, almost dramatic, knock at the door down* L. SALLY *and* ROGER, *startled, look at each other*)

SALLY ⎱
ROGER ⎰ (*together*) Come in.

(JOY AMBLER *walks in down* L. *Or is it more like a stride?* JOY *is not by any means a plain girl, but she gives the impression of being so. She is brisk, efficient and masterful. She wears "practical" clothes, and walks as though she had an imaginary riding-crop in her hand. She carries her handbag*)

JOY. Ah, there you are, Roger. (*She crosses to Roger, putting her handbag on Sally's desk as she passes it*) Found you first shot. Good-oh!
ROGER. Hullo, Joy. (*He holds out his hand*)

(JOY *holds her face up to be kissed.* ROGER, *with a little glance at Sally, pecks Joy's cheek*)

JOY. Now, let's go into your office and talk, shall we?
ROGER. This is my office—my room.
JOY (*looking around*) Great Scott! I imagined a huge desk with hundreds of secretaries—not just one. (*She glances at Sally*)

(SALLY *stiffens*)

ROGER (*hastily*) Oh, Sally isn't my—I mean—Miss Mannering —she is the senior pupil here—Miss Mannering—Miss Ambler.
SALLY (*coldly*) How do you do?
JOY (*coldly*) How do you do?
SALLY (*rising and gathering up some documents*) Excuse me . . .
ROGER. Oh, there's no need . . .
SALLY (*crossing to the door down* R) I have work to do. (*She stops and turns*) And I'm sure you and Miss Ambler have a great deal to discuss.

(SALLY *exits down* R)

JOY. Humph! I'm not sure I like her, Roger.
ROGER. She's really very nice.
JOY. She could be a distraction. And we've got your career to think about. We want you to be a success, don't we?
ROGER (*uncomfortably*) Yes, we do.
JOY (*sitting Roger on the chair* R *of the desk* LC) Work, work, work —that's your programme.
ROGER. Oh, I'm really getting down to it.
JOY (*sitting on the downstage side of the desk* LC) That's my Roger.

Now—I've fixed a couple of things for you—very important.
First, tonight we're having dinner with . . .

ROGER. We?

JOY. You and me, of course.

ROGER. It's a bit awkward. (*He rises and moves* C) As a matter of
fact, I've a rather important case—er—concerns an M.P.

JOY. Which one?

ROGER. I can't tell you that. It would be a breach of pro-
fessional etiquette.

JOY (*briskly*) You can at least give me the outline of the case.
If I'm going to help you in your career, you'll have to get used to
discussing things with me, you know.

ROGER. Er—yes—but it's rather delicate. There's a woman in
it.

JOY. A married woman?

ROGER. Yes, as a matter of fact.

JOY (*rising and moving down* L) Hm—a married woman—sounds
like Mr Pieman.

ROGER (*horrified*) Who did you say?

JOY (*moving to* LC) Pieman. Everyone knows that man's
reputation. Now—the woman—sophisticated type?

ROGER. Yes.

JOY. I know. It's Dorothy Biggs.

ROGER. Oh, Joy—I could get disbarred.

JOY. Nonsense! Do you think I would breathe a word of this
to anyone? (*She advances on Roger*) We're friends, aren't we—
(*archly*) perhaps a little more than friends.

ROGER (*recoiling from her archness*) Oh, yes—(*he backs to the desk* R)
I mean—I've got to work on the case tonight, Joy.

JOY. I've something far more important for you tonight.
Dinner with Uncle George.

ROGER. Uncle George?

JOY (*impatiently*) Uncle George Merivale—the solicitor. One
of the biggest solicitors . . . (*She moves down* C) Oh, Roger—if you
can make a good impression, he'll send you dozens of briefs.

ROGER (*moving to* R *of Joy*) Dozens of . . . Joy! That's marvellous!

JOY. Then you'll come?

ROGER. Well . . .

JOY. Then that's settled. (*She moves to the desk* LC *and sits on it*)
Now, there's something else. Uncle is sending you a brief today.

ROGER. Today—a brief! (*He crosses to* R *of Joy*) Joy, how did
you do it?

JOY. I just gave him his head and over he went.

ROGER. We *are* talking about your uncle?

JOY. Of course we are. Oh, I don't need spurs to ride *him*.
When I told him we were—well—such close friends he was very

interested. Quite excited, really. So tonight I want him to look at the jumps.

ROGER. The jumps?

JOY. You're the jumps, silly. But he's taking the first one blind. Said he'd send you a brief before he saw you. Just to show his confidence.

ROGER. In me?

JOY. In me. (*She rises*) Well, what do you say?

ROGER (*moving* RC) I don't know—I'm overwhelmed.

JOY (*crossing to him*) There's no need to *say* anything.

ROGER. I—er . . .

JOY (*in a low, coy voice*) All I want to do is to make you happy —and successful. (*She suddenly holds up her face, a couple of inches from Roger's, inviting a kiss*)

(ROGER *gives* JOY *a desperate peck. Her answer is to grab him and kiss him.*

GRIMES *enters suddenly up* R.

GREEN *follows him on and lets out a low whistle*)

GRIMES (*recoiling*) Ah—excuse me, my dear fellow—didn't realize you were in conference.

JOY (*calmly*) It's quite all right—I'd just finished.

GRIME (*to Roger*) Well, if you *have* finished—could you step this way a moment?

(ROGER, *embarrassed, hesitates awkwardly between* Joy *and* Grimes)

JOY. I'll see myself out, Roger.

ROGER. Er—yes.

GRIMES. You have finished?

ROGER. Oh, yes. (*He moves to the steps up* R)

GREEN. Looks as though they were just under starter's orders to me.

(GRIMES *and* ROGER *exit up* R.

GREEN *clicks his gums at* JOY, *winks and follows the others off, closing the door behind him.* JOY *crosses to* L *of the desk* LC.

SALLY *enters down* R *and crosses to the desk* LC)

JOY. Roger tells me you're a barrister, too. I think that's marvellous. Not my line of country, though—I'd be stifled in an office. I hope you don't disapprove of my coming here to see Roger.

SALLY. It's not my business.

JOY. I'm glad you see it that way. He has to work, you know. My uncle, George Merivale, the solicitor, thinks Roger will be absolutely brilliant if only he works hard.

SALLY. You can get a fair amount done here—(*she picks up Joy's bag and hands it to her*) if there are not too many interruptions.

JOY (*moving to the door down* L) Well, I know that you won't be a distraction for him at any rate. Good morning. (*She pauses*) Oh, I wonder if you would be kind enough to give Roger a message? Thank you—ask him to collect me about seven-thirty, would you? So nice to have met you, Miss Mannering.

(JOY *exits down* L. *One feels that the first round is with Joy.* SALLY *smacks down a brief in anger.*
BRADLEY, GREEN *and* ROGER *enter up* R)

GREEN (*more or less shoving Bradley across the room*) Come on, young feller-me-lad—best foot forward, stick your neck out . . . (*He moves* C)

(BRADLEY *crosses down* L)

ROGER (*following Green*) But aren't you going to tell me about the case?

GREEN. That's what I like to see. Keenness—enthusiasm— that's the stuff—give it to 'em hot, knock 'em round the ring, no quarter. Another time, old son. Got a couple more calls to make. Tallyho, me boy.

ROGER. But, really . . .

GREEN. Don't worry. All in time. Least said, soonest mended— it's a long lane that has no turning, and what's good keeps. (*To Bradley*) Door!

(BRADLEY *opens the door down* L.
GREEN *exits down* L.
BRADLEY *follows him off*)

ROGER (*eagerly*) Sally, I've got a case . . .

SALLY (*coldly*) How nice.

ROGER. Honestly. That fellow Green. Picked me out—said he wanted someone who looked the part. What did he mean by that?

SALLY. I don't know.

ROGER. Sally, aren't you pleased? My first case—my first case!

(ALEC *enters briskly down* R, *carrying a brief*)

ALEC (*crossing to Roger*) A brief—sent down for you, sir. (*He hands the brief to Roger*)

ROGER (*eagerly*) For me? (*More subdued*) Oh, yes.

ALEC. You were expecting it, sir?

ROGER. In a sort of way—yes.

ALEC. Well, congratulations, sir. The solicitors are Thornton, Merivale and Company.

SALLY. Uncle George.

ALEC. I beg your . . . Oh, I see—old George Merivale—he isn't your uncle, is he, sir?

ROGER. No.

SALLY. Not yet.

ALEC. You follow that up, sir. Thornton, Merivale could make you if they had a mind to. (*He takes out his bag of toffees and offers it to Roger*) Have a toffee, sir.

ROGER. Thanks—er—no, I won't.

ALEC. No? Nothing like a toffee at moments like this. (*He crosses to the door down* R *and turns*) Must say you've taken it very well, Mr Thursby. Young barrister I knew—got his first brief—so overcome he passed out. Smelling salts are in the small cupboard if you get a delayed action, sir.

(ALEC *exits down* R. SALLY *moves up* L *and puts on her coat*)

ROGER (*moving to Sally*) Sally . . .

SALLY (*coldly*) I'm sorry. I didn't congratulate you. Congratulations. Two cases in one morning—you are getting ahead. (*She puts on her hat*)

ROGER. Sally—about tonight . . .

SALLY (*collecting her handbag from the desk drawer*) Oh, didn't I tell you? I can't come. (*She moves to the door down* L) I promised Henry I'd go out with him.

ROGER (*moving below the desk* LC) What about lunch?

SALLY. I'm meeting Henry.

ROGER. Oh.

SALLY. At least you'll be able to have your lunch without any distractions. Oh, by the way. Your lady friend asked me to give you a message. Would you pick her up tonight at seven. Or was it seven-thirty? Make it seven. Mustn't be late for Uncle George. (*She turns to go*)

ROGER. Sally—wait . . .

(SALLY *exits down* L, *slamming the door behind her* ROGER *sinks into the chair* R *of the desk* LC, *with his brief. He looks thoroughly miserable. The telephone rings.* ROGER *lifts the receiver*)

(*Into the telephone. Listlessly*) Yes? . . . Mr Thursby—I'll just see—(*he realizes*) Mr Thursby—oh, yes—speaking . . . Thornton, Merivale . . . Oh, yes . . . I'll be happy to do the case, Mr Merivale . . . Of course, Mr Merivale . . . Conference next week—certainly, Mr Merivale . . . Wednesday, ten a.m. That will be fine . . . Oh, yes—tonight is all laid on, sir—I'm looking forward to it . . . Thank you, Mr Merivale. (*He replaces the receiver, rises, dashes enthusiastically to the desk* R *and notes down the appointment*) "Wednesday, ten a.m. Conference." (*He glances at the brief*) "Newent against Newent—divorce proceedings." (*Almost cheering*) Divorce! (*He sits at the desk* R *and goes eagerly through the brief*)

(MRS THURSBY *enters down* L)

MRS THURSBY (*crossing to Roger*) Roger darling . . .

ROGER (*intent on his brief*) Mmm. (*He half rises and offers his cheek*)

(Mrs Thursby *kisses Roger*)

Oh, hello, Mother. (*He sinks into his chair*)
    Mrs Thursby. Is Kennie—Mr Grimes—in?
    Roger (*too absorbed to look up*) He's in his room, Mother.
Can't attend to you now, dear—I'm frightfully busy.
    Mrs Thursby (*in awe*) Oh—busy . . .
    Roger (*perfunctorily*) Divorce case.

(Mrs Thursby *looks in awe at Roger*)

(*He waves towards the door up* R) You'd better go right in, Mother.

(Mrs Thursby *tiptoes reverently to the steps up* R.
    Grimes *enters up* R)

    Grimes (*on the steps*) Amanda, m'dear—I'm all ready . . .
    Mrs Thursby (*putting her fingers to her lips*) Ssh—sh—Roger's
busy.
    Grimes. Oh.

(Mrs Thursby *takes* Grimes' *hand, and they tiptoe past the
absorbed* Roger *towards the door down* L*. Grimes *is enjoying the
joke*)

    Mrs Thursby (*giving one proud look back at Roger*) It seems only
yesterday that he was in short trousers. And now he's in the
middle of his first divorce.

Mrs Thursby *and* Grimes *exit down* L *as—*

the Curtain *falls*

* (*Alternative* Curtain)

ACT II

Scene—*The same. Wednesday, a few days later.*

When the Curtain rises, Roger is seated at the desk R, busily working on a brief. Sally is seated at the desk LC, speaking on the telephone. Henry enters breezily down L. Sally holds up her finger to show that she is trying to listen.

Sally (*into the telephone*) Yes, Mr Plumb, that's quite right . . . (*To Henry*) Sh!

(Henry *closes the door with exaggerated quietness*)

(*Into the telephone*) It'll be on before Judge Perkins next Friday . . . What's the judge like? Er—well . . . (*She covers the mouthpiece*) Henry—what's Judge Perkins like?

Henry (*from the door*) Bloody awful!

Sally (*into the telephone*) Bl . . . I mean, well, it rather depends . . . Yes, I will, thank you . . . Good-bye. (*She replaces the receiver*) Henry, you might be more helpful.

Henry. I was helpful. He is bloody awful. I thought your translation jolly good. (*He crosses to L of the desk LC*) And now that's over, talk to me.

Sally. I must get on with my work. (*She picks up a brief*)

(Henry *takes the brief and tosses it over his shoulder*)

Henry. *I'm* your work.

Sally. Go away, Henry—you're very nice—but go away.

(Henry *strides across to Roger.* Sally *rises, retrieves the brief and sits at her desk*)

Henry. Well, Roger Thursby, barrister-at-law, have you put in for silk, yet?

Roger. Seriously, Henry, I've got two conferences today.

Henry (*sitting on the upstage end of the desk R*) Have you, by jove! I had to wait a year for one, and then the chap didn't turn up.

Roger. And one of mine is about a defended divorce—defended, Henry. That gives me a chance, doesn't it?

Henry. Gives the other side one, if you ask me. With great respect, old boy, your clients must be mad—unless they want to lose. Who are they?

Roger (*rising; slightly uncomfortable*) Well—as a matter of fact, it's a firm called Thornton, Merivale and Company.

HENRY. Ah, of course, good old Uncle George.

ROGER (*with a glance at Sally*) He isn't my uncle. He happens to be Joy's uncle.

HENRY. That isn't the same thing?

ROGER (*crossing to Sally*) I don't think that's very funny.

HENRY. Neither do I. I think it's damned serious.

ROGER (*ignoring Henry; to Sally*) I'm going to look up something for Grimes, Sally. If my clients arrive, would you mind telling Alex I'm next door?

(ROGER *exits down* L, *slamming the door behind him*)

SALLY. I don't think you should tease him, Henry.

HENRY (*rising and crossing to Sally*) I can't help it. I can't make up my mind whether he's young and innocent— or . . . Never mind, let's talk about us.

SALLY. Or what?

HENRY. I said let's talk about us. Forget Roger. Concentrate on me.

SALLY. I've told you—I have work to do, if you haven't.

HENRY (*putting his hand on top of Sally's documents*) It's all these divorce cases—they're making you cynical. It needn't be like that, Sally. If we got married . . .

SALLY. No.

HENRY (*taking her hand*) I'm serious.

SALLY. Are you? I can never tell.

HENRY (*gently pulling Sally to her feet*) Cross my heart. You whisper the magic word and I'll go to work like a beaver. (*He draws Sally to the bench up* C)

SALLY. If you don't let me get on, I'll say a word, and it won't be "beaver".

(HENRY *and* SALLY *sit on the bench in the window.* HENRY *is* R *of Sally*)

HENRY (*sincerely*) I am serious, Sally. Really. I could work—I would work—if . . . (*He smiles*) In a minute I shall be on my knees to you.

SALLY. Don't you dare.

HENRY. May I ask the conventional question?

SALLY. As long as you don't mind a conventional answer.

HENRY. Is there anyone else in your young life?

SALLY. Who, for instance?

HENRY. Roger, for instance.

SALLY. Of course not . . .

HENRY. Ah, I detect a momentary hesitation—a pause no longer than a heart-beat.

SALLY. Henry, stop pestering! All right, I do like Roger. He makes me furious sometimes—and at others . . .

HENRY. You feel you want to mother him.

SALLY. How did you know?

HENRY. I've seen you looking at him.

SALLY. Does it really show?

HENRY. To a keen observer, yes. (*He breathes in deeply*) The head goes slightly to one side, too—(*he demonstrates*) rather like this.

SALLY. It's ridiculous, really—he's only been here a few days.

HENRY. Absolutely ridiculous.

SALLY (*touching his hand*) You really are awfully nice.

HENRY. Thank you. And now comes the line about you and me being friends for the rest of our lives. I know the dialogue.

(*Underneath his bantering manner,* HENRY *is really quite hurt and upset, and* SALLY *senses it*)

SALLY. If only you'd work . . .

HENRY (*sincerely*) To what end? Or should it be—to which end? Doesn't matter. (*Cheerfully*) Lunch? (*He rises*)

SALLY (*rising*) All right. Usual table.

(HENRY *kisses Sally.*
ROGER *enters down* L. SALLY *goes to her desk*)

ROGER (*crossing to* R *of Henry*) Blagrove—that remark you made about Miss Ambler's uncle just before I went out . . .

HENRY. You've been churning it over, have you? Good.

ROGER (*stiffly*) I resent the implication behind your remark.

HENRY. It was just a sort of smoke-signal, old boy.

ROGER. Smoke-signal? What for?

HENRY. Lord, this is too deep for me. (*He crosses to the door down* L) You tell him, Sally. Sorry, old chap—got to go and see a client.

ROGER. Just a moment . . .

HENRY. Hell—I *do* have an occasional client, you know. And don't be so bloody pompous.

(HENRY *stalks out down* L)

SALLY (*moving to* R *of the desk* LC) You deserved that.

ROGER. What did he mean about a smoke-signal?

SALLY. I don't know, really—you mustn't take Henry seriously.

ROGER. Was I pompous?

SALLY. A bit.

ROGER. Lord—that's the last thing . . . Sally, if I ever sound pompous to you, will you tell me?

SALLY. I'll kick your shin.

ROGER. Not too hard.

SALLY. That will depend on how pompous you are.

ROGER (*seriously*) Sally, why doesn't Henry do better? I mean —he could get any amount of work if he tried.

SALLY (*moving to Roger*) Excuse me. (*She kicks Roger's shin*)

(ROGER *yells.* SALLY *goes to her desk and sits.*
    GRIMES *enters up* R)

GRIMES. Anything the matter, m'dear fellow?
ROGER. Ooh—no.
GRIMES. Rheumatism? These chambers are draughty.
ROGER. I'm all right. Er—I looked up that point you asked me about.
GRIMES. Ah, good. And what did ye find out?
ROGER. I looked it up first of all in *Halsbury.*
GRIMES. That's right, m'dear fellow, that's the way.

(GRIMES *crosses to* SALLY *and starts to discuss something with her. The following speeches by* ROGER *and* GRIMES *are run together, with* GRIMES *speaking softly to Sally, and occasionally breaking off to talk to Roger.* ROGER *does the "barrister act" until he notices* GRIMES *is apparently not listening*)

ROGER
GRIMES   (*together*)

It said that if you charged a crime in a civil action it has to be proved, just as fully as it would have to be in a criminal court . . .

Look, Sally—in this case of Barnes—I'm a bit worried about the warranty claim. Can ye find me a case where an oral warranty has been . . . (*He breaks off, noticing that Roger has stopped*) Go on, m'dear fellow, I can hear ye.

ROGER
GRIMES   (*together*)

. . . as it would be in a criminal court, that is to say, beyond all reasonable doubt.

(*To Sally*) I was saying—can ye find me a case where an oral warranty has been proved in spite of the fact that the parties had signed the R.I.B.A. contract? (*He notices Roger has stopped*) Go on, m'dear fellow.

ROGER (*slightly annoyed*) I didn't want to interrupt.
GRIMES (*firmly*) Now look, m'dear fellow—ye'll have to addresss a judge one day, and if ye stop every time ye think he isn't listening to ye, ye'll never get started.
ROGER. I'm sorry.

(ALEC *enters down* R)

GRIMES. Ah, no—never be sorry. No good with witnesses. Be angry—be glad—be jovial—be solemn—be perplexed—be struck dumb even—but never, never be sorry. Ye make *them* sorry, m'dear fellow, that's the way.
ALEC (*crossing to the door down* L) If we don't get across the road,

someone else is going to be sorry. Master Tiptree's waiting for you.

GRIMES. Dear, dear—that'll never do. (*To Roger*) Aren't ye coming with us?

ROGER. I've got a conference as a matter of fact.

GRIMES. Already? Well, well, well—they will do these things, they will do 'em. (*He crosses hurriedly to the door down* L)

(GREEN *and* BRADLEY *enter down* L *and almost collide with* GRIMES)

GREEN. Hallo, hallo, hallo—where's the fire?

GRIMES. Excuse me, m'dear fellow.

(GRIMES *exits down* L.
  ALEC *follows him off*)

GREEN (*looking after Grimes*) Blimey, he keeps fit for an old 'un. (*He crosses to Roger*) Well, we all ship-shape and Bristol fashion? Ready for a chin-wag, eh?

(ROGER *moves to his desk* R *and sits*)

ROGER (*formally*) All ready, Mr Green. Won't you sit down?

SALLY (*rising and moving to* L *of Green*) I've one or two things to look up in the library.

GREEN. No, don't go, miss. Like to have a bit of glamour around when I'm working. Gives me uplift. (*To Bradley*) You sit down—(*he points up* C) over there and read your comic, Mr Bradley.

(BRADLEY *crosses to the bench up* C, *sits, takes a comic from his pocket and reads it.* SALLY *perches on the right end of her desk*)

(*He sits* L *of the desk* R) Now, Mr Thursby. I've got it all laid on— tell you what we'll do—this'll be a bit of cake.

ROGER. I thought *I* was appearing for *you*.

GREEN. I know, I know. But you haven't had the experience I've had. I got to steer you right. Do you know that I was once charged on an indictment containing thirty-three counts? Not bad, eh? That's treating a chap with proper respect.

SALLY. What happened?

GREEN. Never mind what happened—that's not the point. Thirty-three was my record. I've had a twenty-five, a twenty, and never less than ten or twelve. And then *this* comes along. I ask you, is it fair? Is it reasonable? They come up with one count— one solitary, miserable count—at my time of life. It hurts. I tell you this—I very nearly decided to plead guilty and be done with it. And I've never pleaded guilty before, not in the whole of my career.

ROGER. What made you decide against it?

GREEN. Thought it might interfere with Ascot. But if it hadn't been for that—well, I'd have cut the ground from under their feet. "Guilty", I should have said. Green pleading guilty—it would have shaken 'em to the core.

ROGER (*coughing*) Now look, Mr Green—I know I'm new to the Bar, but you're paying me to help you . . .

GREEN. You'll do well. You think of essentials. Let's get down to brass tacks. No beating about the bush. All fair and above board. In for a penny, in for a pound. Who laughs last, laughs loudest. Did you say you couldn't sing—or you could? I don't remember.

ROGER (*with a look at Sally*) Mr Green—please don't think I'm meaning to be offensive—but have you ever thought of pleading —that is—I mean—putting up a defence of insanity?

GREEN. Cheer up. I always do this to begin with. Helps me to find out what sort of chap you are. (*He rises and moves* C) Now, look—there's only one count against me. One count—we're as good as out in the road already. Only we're not. But we shall be.

ROGER. Obtaining money by false pretences with intent to defraud.

GREEN. Ridiculous. Laughable. Ha-ha!

SALLY. Ha-ha!

BRADLEY. Ha!

GREEN. Thank you, Mr Bradley. It won't stick—they'll never wear it.

ROGER. Hadn't we better go into the facts?

GREEN (*moving to the desk* R) Facts? What d'you want to go into them for? I was enjoying myself—(*he glances at Bradley*) so was he.

ROGER (*doggedly*) I haven't seen a copy of the depositions yet. Have you got them?

GREEN. That's a fair question. (*He turns and winks at Sally*) Here's a fair answer—yes.

ROGER. Can I see them, please?

GREEN (*leaning over the desk to Roger*) Don't you think it might put you off?

(SALLY *rises and moves* C)

ROGER (*angrily*) Mr Green—if you're not mad and you want me to defend you, you must let me see the depositions.

GREEN (*banging on the desk*) At last! Only say it louder next time. Don't you understand that at your game you've got to be able to shout down the other side?

ROGER. Now—really . . .

GREEN. What hope have you got if you can't shout me down, eh? (*He turns to Sally*) I ask you, miss—what chance has he got?

SALLY. I think you're being rather hard on Mr Thursby.

GREEN. You got to be cruel to be kind. Otherwise he'll never learn. It's taken me ten minutes to get him annoyed. (*He turns to Roger*) Now, come on—get tough—let's see some rough stuff.

C

ROGER. All right—perhaps you'd tell me what it's all about in as few words as possible, please.

GREEN. Apart from the "please", that was all right.

ROGER (*rising; angrily*) What is it all about?

GREEN. Good—good—better. (*He sits on the chair* L *of the desk* R) Toffee.

ROGER (*resuming his seat*) No, thanks.

GREEN. No, no, no. I'm not offering—I'm telling. I run a postal business, see—selling toffee.

SALLY (*crossing and standing above the desk* R) Selling toffee—by *post?*

GREEN. Nothing wrong with that, is there?

SALLY. Not if the customers get enough toffee for their money.

GREEN. She's quick, y'know—she'll bear watching. As a matter of fact, miss, they didn't. But I'm not charged with that.

ROGER. Would it trouble you too much to tell me what you *are* charged with?

GREEN. All in good time. Now, listen—you've got to follow this. First—I advertise toffee for sale—get that?

ROGER. Got it.

GREEN. Second, when they write and order toffee, I always send 'em a nice little testimonial. Just in case they're worried about the quality of the goods. Got that?

ROGER. I've got that.

GREEN. Good. It's a very nice little testimonial, actually. (*He rises*) Here—listen. (*He takes a letter from his pocket, stands on the steps up* R *and reads*) "I have known Mr Green and eaten his toffee for over twenty years. I can thoroughly recommend both of them. Made only from the purest ingredients, the toffee will not only give pleasure to one and all, but it also wards off coughs, chills and influenza." That's good, y'know—modest and yet becoming —like myself.

SALLY. Of course, Mr Green.

ROGER. I am still waiting to . . .

GREEN. The charge? Well, I told you—it's ridiculous. I'm accused of forging that reference. Blind Freddie can see that it's signed "G. St Clair Smith". See for yourself. (*He hands the letter to Roger*)

ROGER. G. St Clair Smith. Is there such a person?

GREEN (*sitting* L *of the desk* R) No idea. There may be, for all I know.

ROGER. Then who did write the reference?

GREEN. Who do you think?

ROGER. Well, if you ask me to be frank, I think you did.

GREEN. Don't be bashful about it. Of course I did.

ROGER. Well—if you wrote yourself a reference and pretended that it was written by Mr Smith—what's your defence?

GREEN (*rising and moving* C) You are making me work. My

defence is that they ordered the toffee before they saw the reference.

ROGER. You had cash from these people?

GREEN. Certainly.

SALLY. And you sent them the toffee?

GREEN. Certainly.

ROGER. How much?

GREEN. At least a quarter of what they ordered. More like a third.

SALLY. But you got the full price?

GREEN. Certainly.

ROGER. Sounds pretty fishy to me.

GREEN. Well, of course it's fishy. I wouldn't be here if it wasn't fishy. But that doesn't mean it's a crime. Oh, dear, no. This feller who's complaining wants his toffee badly. Got a sweet tooth. Doesn't wait for the reference. He sends the money—and I send him the toffee.

ROGER. You *didn't* send him a reference, then?

GREEN. Oh, yes. I always like 'em to read St Clair's letter. That's literature. I sent him a copy of the testimonial at the same time as I sent the toffee.

ROGER. Wait a minute! If he didn't see the testimonial before he sent the money, then he wasn't influenced by it. He decided to buy without reading the reference.

GREEN. He's bright. He'll get there.

ROGER. Let me see the indictment.

(GREEN *hands a document to* ROGER *who peruses it.* SALLY *reads it over Roger's shoulder*)

Just a moment—this says that your client received the testimonial *before* he sent the money.

GREEN (*blandly*) Naturally.

SALLY. I'm a little confused . . .

GREEN. No need for that. It's dead simple. (*He takes out his wallet*) Hey, presto! (*He extracts a receipt and hands it to Roger*) What's this?

ROGER. A receipt for posting a letter.

GREEN. Good for you. Proof of posting a letter containing the testimonial. And what's this? (*He hands over another receipt*)

ROGER. Receipt for despatch of one crate of toffee. (*He compares the receipts*) Both dated the ninth of July.

GREEN. There's your proof.

SALLY. But why does the customer think he received the testimonial before ordering the toffee?

GREEN. Because I put an earlier date on the letter.

ROGER. Why?

GREEN. Because I wanted him to think he'd had it earlier, that's why.

ROGER. I don't follow . . .

GREEN (*kindly*) Don't try, son. You stick to the facts. You just wave these things under the judge's nose—that's all.

ROGER. You don't need me . . .

GREEN. Oh, yes, I do. Feller always needs a good defence counsel. (*He rises*) You got the right looks—you're new—a judge will always be sympathetic to a new bloke, see? Well—I got to scarper. (*He whistles to Bradley*) Come on, Mr Bradley. (*He moves* C)

(BRADLEY *rises and crosses to the door down* L)

ROGER (*rising*) Wait . . .

GREEN. Not to worry, Mr Thursby. You just be grateful—you've got a winning case. 'Bye. (*To Bradley*) Door!

(BRADLEY *opens the door down* L.
    GREEN *sweeps out down* L.
    BRADLEY *follows him off*)

ROGER. Sally—I don't understand a word of it.

SALLY. I think I do.

ROGER. Do you really? Can you make me understand it?

SALLY (*moving* C) I'll try.

ROGER (*crossing to Sally*) You're an angel. Will I want a cold compress?

SALLY. Sit down. (*She sits Roger in the chair* R *of the desk* LC *and puts her hand on his forehead*) Will this do, instead?

ROGER. That's wonderful. (*He pauses*) Wonderful. (*He pauses*) But seriously, Sally, I do want to know what it's all about.

(SALLY *looks lovingly at Roger*)

About Green, I mean.

SALLY. Yes, of course, Green. (*She sits at her desk*) Well, Mr Green runs phoney businesses. He advertises goods for sale, gets the money and either doesn't send the goods, or sends only a quarter of them. D'you understand so far?

ROGER. I think so.

SALLY. Well, every so often people who've been cheated complain to the police and they call on Mr Green and prosecute him for fraud.

ROGER. What's the fraud?

SALLY. Not having a genuine business and getting money by pretending that he has.

ROGER. But they haven't charged him with that this time.

SALLY. That's the point. He's made them think there's a much simpler cast-iron charge. You see, to prove he hasn't a genuine business involves quite a lot of work. And so Mr Green provides them with an obviously forged reference.

ROGER. But where does that get him? He'll have to admit he forged the reference.

SALLY. But forgery of a letter by itself isn't a crime, and Green knows it. The police have got to show he got the money because of the forgery. And they can't do that because he sent it after he got the money.

ROGER. Why did he put an earlier date on it?

SALLY. So as to make the police and the customer *think* it was sent before. But it wasn't sent before the toffee, and he'll be able to prove it when the time comes.

ROGER. I see.

SALLY. Good.

ROGER (*rising and moving* C) The only thing that still troubles me is that he seemed disappointed there was only one charge against him.

SALLY. Oh, Roger, his name's Green, not yours.

(GREEN *enters down* L. SALLY *rises*)

GREEN. I forgot to ask you—how d'you like the whistle—the suit?

ROGER. Very nice.

GREEN. Miss? A female opinion . . .

SALLY. Just the right touch—modest and yet becoming—rather like you, Mr Green.

GREEN. It's a pleasure to do business with a firm like yours. You see—I thought I'd wear this in court. I'm playing the leading part, and I've got to be dressed for it. Cost over twenty nicker, this did.

ROGER. Proceeds of the toffee business?

GREEN. More or less. One other thing, sir. Sometimes my heart plays me up. (*He collapses on the desk* LC *then recovers very quickly*) If I'm took queer on the day of the trial, I shall want you to ask for an adjournment.

ROGER. But—I say—really . . .

GREEN. I don't fight unless I'm one hundred per cent fit. It's all right for you—but I'm the one who's got to go into the witness-box and lie like a trooper.

ROGER. You're not going to commit perjury!

GREEN (*crossing to the door down* L) Just a manner of speaking. I shall tell them more truth than I gave them toffee. Ta-ta.

ROGER (*crossing to Green*) Wait. Mr Green—you don't seem to realize—you *will* tell the truth, won't you?

GREEN. Honestly—to hear you talk anyone would think I was a crook.

(GREEN *exits down* L. ROGER *and* SALLY *look at each other for a moment, and then laugh.* SALLY *moves up* C)

ROGER (*smiling*) Well, I hope the judge will understand it. *I* don't.

SALLY. I think the only one who understands it is Mr Green. I should leave it to him.

(ALEC *pops his head round the door down* L)

ALEC. Mr Blagrove? No?
SALLY. He was in here a few moments ago. Don't know where he went.
ALEC. Mmm. Must have gone out. If you see him before I do, tell him I've just had a brief sent down for him, will you?

(ALEC *withdraws*)

SALLY. You know, you should smile more often. Like you did just now. It made the whole room look brighter. You take everything so seriously.
ROGER (*moving to* R *of Sally*) I don't usually. I expect it's because it's all so new. I'm worried—I can't afford to make a hash of things.
SALLY. You won't. But don't try any short cuts, either, please.
ROGER. I wish I knew some.

(SALLY *gives Roger a quick glance*)

SALLY (*kneeling on the bench up* C) It's none of my business, anyway.
ROGER. What isn't?
SALLY (*sitting on the bench up* C) You—and any short cuts you may have in mind.
ROGER (*sitting* R *of Sally on the bench*) But I said I . . . Sally, what are you getting at?
SALLY (*smiling*) Forget it.
ROGER. I wish I *were* your business.
SALLY. Do you now?
ROGER. I mean—I do admire you and all that—I need your advice and help. Sally, would you have dinner tonight?
SALLY. Do you remember what happened last time you asked me?
ROGER. It won't happen again. I promise. I've a million questions to ask you. Say "yes".
SALLY. Yes. All right. Providing we only talk shop for half the evening.
ROGER. And the other half?
SALLY. Let's feel free to enjoy ourselves, shall we?

(*They share a laugh again*)

ROGER. It's a date, then.

(ROGER *rises and holds out his hand.* SALLY *takes Roger's hand and rises. They shake hands for a moment in mock solemnity and then, looking at each other, the mood changes. They are drawn towards each other)*

Sally—darling . . .

SALLY. Yes?

ROGER. I—you see—I mean . . . You have the most beautiful eyes, did you know that?

SALLY. Go on, Mr Thursby.

ROGER. I could fall in love with you terribly easily.

SALLY. Yes?

(*They are very close. They waver before each other, a hair's-breadth away from a kiss*)

ROGER (*jumping back*) No, I mustn't.

SALLY (*moving to her desk LC; half angry and disappointed*) Joy?

ROGER (*moving to R of Sally's desk*) Joy? Heavens—she's got nothing to do with it. Sally—darling—you have a tremendous attraction for me.

SALLY. Thank you.

ROGER. But—you see—when a girl has sort of been in my arms, I go on thinking about it. It multiplies.

SALLY. And who has sort of been in your arms? I haven't.

ROGER. No—you see—that's why—I want to have you there— but if I did—I'd never get any work done at all—it would go on multiplying—and multiplying . . .

SALLY. It sounds wonderful.

ROGER (*moving C*) I've got to be firm. Sally, you do understand, don't you? Loving you would be a full-time job. And the Bar is a whole-time job, too. I haven't time for both.

SALLY (*smiling*) You're going all serious again, my poppet.

ROGER. I must seem like an awful clot.

SALLY. A clot. But not so awful.

ROGER. And you will help me?

SALLY. If I see you multiplying anything, I'll kick your other shin.

ROGER (*tenderly*) You really are wonderful. (*He moves towards her*)

(SALLY *lifts her foot to kick him*)

SALLY. Careful! Remember—you are married to your career.

(ROGER *smiles and stops. They look at each other, then* ROGER *moves towards Sally. There is a knock at the door down* L. ROGER *moves* RC *and clears his throat*)

ROGER (*calling*) Come in.

(JOY *enters hurriedly down* L. *She wears an engagement ring. She gives a quick glance at Sally and Roger*)

(*He moves above his desk* R. *With forced heartiness*) Joy—oh, Joy! Come on in. (*He sits at the desk*)

JOY (*crossing to* C) Roger, darling—I've only a moment. I want to speak to you urgently. In private.

SALLY. I'll go to the library.

JOY. Thank you.

SALLY. Not at all. (*She picks up some papers, moves to the door down* L *and turns*) I shall be gone some time. Just in case you get any multiplication problems, Roger.

    (SALLY *exits down* L)

JOY. What did she mean by that?

ROGER. Mmm? Oh—a private joke.

JOY. I don't like that woman, Roger. The sooner you get a room of your own the better. Roger—Uncle George is on his way here.

ROGER (*trying to be busy*) I know. I have a conference with him and a client in a few moments.

JOY (*moving to* L *of the desk* R) I had to talk to you before he came. You see the most wonderful thing has happened. I heard uncle talking to his clerk about a very important action for Baggally's, the big store. They were saying something about having an extra junior. His fees would be four hundred guineas.

ROGER (*rising*) Four hundred!

JOY. And refreshers of about a hundred guineas a day. If the case lasts about six weeks as they seem to think—it would come to between three and four thousand pounds.

ROGER. It'll be a few years before I get that sort of money. Three thousand pounds—phew!

JOY (*sitting in the chair* L *of the desk* R) I wasn't supposed to be listening—but I heard it all and I said to myself—"An extra junior—why not Roger?" Why not? No responsibility and all that money.

ROGER. You didn't say that to your uncle?

JOY. I certainly did. *I've* never refused a jump yet.

ROGER. Good Lord! What did he do—laugh?

JOY. At first—yes. And that made me damn angry. I told him it was the least he could do for someone who was practically a member of the family.

ROGER (*startled*) Practically a . . .

JOY. That pulled him up short, I can tell you.

ROGER. It pulled me up, too.

JOY. And when I told him that you and I were more or less engaged . . .

ROGER. But—Joy . . .

JOY. I had to, Roger. Don't you see? (*She rises and moves to* R *of the desk* LC) That clinched it. He is going to offer you the brief. That's why I had to see you.

ROGER (*crossing to* R *of Joy*) But it isn't true, Joy. I mean—we're not—are we?

JOY (*backing Roger to* L *of the desk* R) I couldn't let the chance go just because of a technicality, darling. I mean—I'm no fool. You were going to ask me, weren't you? Come on, now, admit it.

ROGER. Well . . .

JOY (*linking her arm through his*) There you are, then. I knew it was just a question of time. Uncle is jolly pleased, I can tell you. I pulled his leg about it—"Uncle", I said, "anyone would think you were glad to get rid of me."

ROGER (*weakly*) What did he say?

JOY. Oh, he laughed. (*She crosses briskly to* LC) Now, I won't hold you up any longer. When uncle comes you can accept his offer with a clear conscience. And we're meeting for dinner to-night to discuss all the other arrangements.

ROGER (*with a step towards her*) Other arrangements?

JOY (*fondly*) The wedding—idiot! But don't worry. I'll do everything. I know you don't believe in long engagements—neither do I. Leave it to me, darling. (*She advances to him for a kiss*) Kiss . . .

ROGER (*desperately*) Joy—listen—please . . .

JOY. Later—later. Head down now—work. (*She kisses him*)

(ROGER *is too stunned to resist*)

(*She crosses to the door down* L *and turns*) Oh, by the way—I knew you'd be too busy. So I bought a ring. Like it? (*She extends her left hand on which there flashes an engagement ring*)

ROGER. You bought it?

JOY. Don't worry. You can pay for it out of your fees on the new case. And I told Uncle George a white lie. I said you'd bought it. I bet you're surprised.

ROGER. Overwhelmed!

JOY. I know it seems unromantic—but after all, that can come later. What do you say to Paris for the honeymoon, eh?

ROGER (*gulping*) Paris . . . (*He slumps into the chair* L *of the desk* R)

JOY. Knew that would get you. I want to try and arrange it for next month. There's a big Horse-of-the-Year show on then—nothing like killing two birds with one stone, eh?

(JOY *exits breezily down* L. ROGER *looks towards the door, speechless.*

JOY *re-enters.*

GEORGE MERIVALE *follows her on.* MERIVALE *is a plumpish, cheerful solicitor*)

There he is, Uncle. All ready for you.

(ROGER *sits up, trying to gather his forces*)

(*She blows a kiss to Roger*) I'll leave you men together, then.

(Joy *exits down* L. Merivale *advances on* Roger, *who rises*)

Merivale. Well, well, well! You've done it, you young dog. Congratulations.

(Merivale *shakes* Roger's *limp hand*)

Roger. Actually, sir, I think I ought to explain.

Merivale. Couldn't believe it until I saw the ring. That clinched it. Great relief to me, I can tell you. (*Hastily*) Not that I want to see her go, of course.

Roger. Of course not.

Merivale (*sitting on the chair* R *of the desk* LC) Y'know, I've no children of my own. Joy is pretty well a daughter to me. My pleasure is giving her what she wants. I hope you understand me, young man?

Roger. I think so.

Merivale. Good. You happen to be what she wants. A bright young man, full of fight, determined to get on. Very good. No reason why business can't be combined with pleasure, eh? Do we still understand one another?

Roger. Yes, but you see . . .

Merivale. Capital! No reason why I can't put a good deal of work in your way, my boy. As a matter of fact, I've something pretty big up my sleeve just now—dare say Joy mentioned it.

Roger. Yes, she did. I wanted to . . .

Merivale (*rather pained*) My boy, do you mind if I make a criticism?

Roger. Not at all.

Merivale. I've noticed it before. You haven't yet learned to let the other man finish speaking. You will interrupt . . .

Roger. I'm very sorry.

Merivale. There you go again. You see? You must learn to read the signs. Very important at the Bar. Every speaker has his own method of showing he's finished. Some purse their lips like this—(*he demonstrates*) some use their hands like this—(*he demonstrates*) some lean back like this (*he demonstrates*). Every man has his own idiosyncrasies.

Roger. Mr Merivale—I must explain . . .

Merivale. Ah, ah, ah! There you go again. Did I purse my lips? Did I use my hands? Did I do anything to make you think I'd finished speaking?

Roger. Yes, sir. You stopped.

Merivale (*patiently*) My boy, speech consists of words *and* pauses. I hadn't stopped. I merely paused.

(Roger *opens his mouth to speak, but checks himself*)

That's better—you recognized it that time. Now, to get back to the other business. We wouldn't normally consider a young man of your limited experience, but as my niece said—since you are practically a member of the family . . .

(ALEC *enters down* L *and crosses to* LC)

ALEC. Your client is here, sir. Good morning, Mr Merivale.

MERIVALE (*rising and moving to* R *of Alec*) Good morning, Alec. How's the fishing?

ALEC. I've not done too well this season.

MERIVALE. I'd like to come along with you one day. Used to be pretty good at it.

ALEC. Didn't know you had time for fishing, sir.

MERIVALE (*rubbing his hands together; jovially*) Oh, I haven't, in the past. (*He moves* C) But thanks to this young man, I hope to have more time in the future. (*He slaps Roger on the back*) Eh, Roger?

ROGER (*miserably*) Er—yes.

MERIVALE. You did a great thing for our firm when you took in Mr Thursby, Alec—splendid! Well, shall we see the lady, Roger?

ROGER. Yes—er—please show her in, Alec.

ALEC. Right, sir.

(ALEC *gives Roger a curious look, then exits down* L)

MERIVALE. I shall leave it all to you, my boy. It'll be a pleasure to watch you in action. (*He moves up* C)

ROGER. Thank you, sir. (*He sets the chair* L *of his desk ready for the client*)

(ALEC *enters down* L *and stands to one side*)

ALEC (*announcing*) Mrs Newent, sir.

(MRS NEWENT *enters down* L. *She is attractive in a cheap sort of way, rather over-dressed and wears too much make-up. She has shapely legs which she takes care to display during the ensuing scene*)

MERIVALE. Come in, Mrs Newent.

(MRS NEWENT *crosses to* C)

Let me introduce you to your counsel, Mr Thursby. Mr Roger Thursby.

(ALEC *crosses above the others and exits down* R)

ROGER. How do you do?

MRS NEWENT (*approvingly*) How do you do?

ROGER (*indicating the chair* L *of his desk*) Won't you sit down?

MRS NEWENT. Thank you, I'm sure. (*She sits* L *of the desk* R *and crosses her knees*)

(ROGER *clears his throat rather officially*)

(*She gets in first*) You're rather young. Still, I don't mind. I feel sort of safe with you.

ROGER. Thank you.

(ROGER *is caught looking at* MRS NEWENT's *legs. She catches his eye and smiles.* ROGER *coughs hurriedly and looks away. There is a pause.* MERIVALE *coughs impatiently*)

Mmm—mmm . . .

MRS NEWENT (*encouragingly*) Yes?

ROGER. Mmm—er—it's very good of you to come.

MRS NEWENT. Well, that's the least I could do, seeing that I want a divorce, isn't it?

ROGER. Quite. (*He looks at her legs, looks at Merivale, then moves quickly behind his desk, sits and shuffles his papers*)

MRS NEWENT. Oh, I do believe he's shy. Isn't that nice?

MERIVALE (*moving above the desk* R) Wasn't there something you wanted to ask Mrs Newent, Mr Thursby?

MRS NEWENT. Now don't rush the poor lamb. I'm quite comfy. No hurry.

ROGER. Er—mmm—yes, there were one or two questions.

MRS NEWENT. Yes?

ROGER. I just—er—(*he shuffles his papers*) I have them here.

MERIVALE (*in a hoarse whisper*) Discretion statement.

ROGER. Mmm? Oh, yes. It's about your discretion statement, Mrs Newent?

MRS NEWENT. Mr Merivale wrote that out. I only signed it. That's right, isn't it, Mr Merivale?

MERIVALE. I wrote it out on your instructions, Mrs Newent.

MRS NEWENT. I don't remember giving any instructions.

MERIVALE. It is what you told me. (*He gets the chair* R *of the desk* LC, *puts it* C *in line with Mrs Newent and sits*)

MRS NEWENT. Oh, yes. What long words you lawyers use. If you'd said that at first, I'd have known at once. (*She smiles at Roger*)

ROGER. Er—mm—I take it the statement is true, Mrs Newent?

MRS NEWENT (*smiling*) I'm not in the habit of telling fibs, you know.

ROGER. Of course, I didn't mean . . .

MRS NEWENT. Then what did you mean?

ROGER. I—er—perhaps we could go through it.

MRS NEWENT. If it's any help.

ROGER (*referring to his papers*) You—er—committed—I mean—according to the statement, you were—you did . . .

MERIVALE (*firmly*) According to your statement, you committed adultery on only one occasion—and you are asking for the discretion of the court—in regard to that one occasion.

MRS NEWENT. You ought to know—you wrote it out.

ROGER. That is—ah—the point. Only once.

Mrs Newent. Once.

Roger. And on that occasion you'd had a little too much to drink.

Mrs Newent. You should've seen me. Gin-and-French's all the evening. I felt on top of the world.

Roger. It says here you became dizzy and faint.

Mrs Newent. That's right.

Roger. After you felt on top of the world you became dizzy and faint?

Mrs Newent. That's it exactly! I'm glad I've got you. D'you mind if I have a smoke?

Roger. Oh, of course not. (*He rises, takes his cigarettes from his pocket and moves below the desk to Mrs Newent). Allow me. (He offers her his case*)

(Mrs Newent *takes a cigarette.* Roger *lights it for her. She guides his hand to the cigarette, smiling up at him.* Merivale *coughs*)

Mrs Newent. You'll do well, I'm sure. You've got the looks for one thing. Mark my words, we'll see your name in the Sunday papers before you're much older.

(Roger *coughs, moves behind his desk and sits*)

Roger. Well, now. About this—er—occasion—on which you —er—you are quite sure your husband knew nothing about it?

(Mrs Newent *puts a finger to the side of her nose and winks*)

Quite. But are you sure?

Mrs Newent. He hadn't a notion. We were discretion itself— (*she laughs*) if you'll pardon the word.

Roger. But how could you have been discretion itself if you were faint and dizzy?

Mrs Newent. Really—you're not as clever as I thought. I go to a dance—right?

Roger. Yes.

Mrs Newent. I drink too much. Right?

Roger. Yes.

Mrs Newent. I go out into the cold air—and as every judge knows, I should hope—it hits me for six. Right?

Roger. You became faint and dizzy.

Mrs Newent. Faint and dizzy. So he helps me home.

Roger. He? Oh, yes—the—er—other party. ·

Mrs Newent. Good. Now I'm home. I'm still faint and dizzy at the bottom of the stairs. Can't get up by myself. Right?

Roger. Yes.

Mrs Newent. He helps me up the stairs. We get to my room. Still faint and dizzy. Are you with me?

Roger. Oh, yes. You're in the bedroom—I'm with you. I mean, he's with you.

MRS NEWENT. So far he has behaved like a perfect gent. When we get to the bedroom we take a liking to each other.

ROGER. You are still faint and dizzy?

MRS NEWENT. No—it had passed off a bit. But it was too late.

ROGER. Too late?

MRS NEWENT (*snorting*) Honestly! We were in the bedroom!

ROGER. Yes—I see. But how did you know that your husband knew nothing of what was going—er—on?

MRS NEWENT. Because he wasn't there, and no-one told him.

ROGER (*rising*) I see. (*He moves above the desk to* C) How—er—long did—(*he darts to the desk and consults his papers*) Bert stay with you? (*He crosses above Mrs Newent to* L *of her*)

MRS NEWENT. Tell the truth, I don't know. I was asleep when he went. But I know he was ever so careful.

ROGER. When did your husband come back?

MRS NEWENT. Oh, it was late.

ROGER. And Bert had gone?

MRS NEWENT. Of course. Would I be sitting here telling you this if we'd been caught?

ROGER. No—I suppose not. (*He moves above his desk and leans on it*) Was there anything in your husband's manner to suggest that he suspected anything?

MRS NEWENT. Not a thing. He was the same as ever. Cold as an iceberg. I mean—a woman's got to get a bit of warmth from someone, hasn't she?

(ROGER *reacts and crosses to* C)

ROGER. Yes. I see. It *was* only once?

MRS NEWENT (*with emphasis*) It was only the once. Because I know what's nice, that doesn't mean to say I don't know what's wrong. (*She rises*) Now—what else do you want to know? I'm getting a bit tired of this—I thought you were on my side.

ROGER. I am on your side—but I have to ask you these questions.

MRS NEWENT (*moving down* RC) I can't see why. It's all plain and straightforward. The man treated me . . . Well—it's all there, in the papers. He deserted me. Why don't you concentrate on that, instead of asking me a lot of intimate questions?

MERIVALE (*rising and replacing his chair* R *of the desk* LC) We have a duty to the court—we have to make sure that your—er—discretion will stand up.

MRS NEWENT (*crossing below Roger to* R *of Merivale; in rising anger*) You wouldn't have known anything about it if I hadn't told you. That's what you get for being honest.

ROGER. We appreciate that, Mrs Newent.

MRS NEWENT. Do you? All this fuss? I went with my friend the other day. She got her divorce in five minutes. (*She clicks her fingers*) Like that. She didn't put in any discretion statement,

either—no fear. She couldn't have remembered for one thing.
I should have kept my mouth shut. It's not as though I'd done
anything really wrong.

Roger. There *was* this one occasion . . .

Mrs Newent. All right, all right, all right. Don't keep harping
on it. Haven't you ever kicked over the traces? (*Doubtfully*) No,
I don't suppose you have. All right, I was wrong to let him come
to my room that night. All right, I've told you. There it is in
black and white. You've got my discretion statement and I hope
it chokes you both—and the judge. (*She crosses to the door down* L)
And now, if there's nothing else—I've better things to do.

(Roger *looks unhappy, but can only make noises*)

No? Right.

(Mrs Newent *exits down* L, *slamming the door after her*)

Roger (*moving to* R *of Merivale*) I don't think I handled that
very well, sir.

Merivale. She was rather difficult. You might have been a
little firmer. Still, that will come, in time. I think it might help
if you were to pop into the Divorce Court and see how some of
the cases are handled—a great deal can depend on the judge, you
know.

Roger. I'll do that, sir.

Merivale. Good. Now, I must go. (*He crosses to the door down* L)
We're meeting tonight, don't forget. I've ordered champagne—a
few friends are coming in—we'll make a nice dignified announcement.

Roger. Announcement?

Merivale. About you and Joy, my boy.

Roger. Oh! Look, sir, before you go . . .

Merivale. Haven't time now, my boy. I'll tell you all about
that other surprise tonight, as well. We shall go a long way together, a long way.

(Mrs Thursby *enters down* L)

(*He moves aside*) Excuse me, madam.

Mrs Thursby. I'm sorry, Roger—didn't mean to interrupt
you.

Merivale. I was just going—er . . .

Roger. This is my mother, sir. Mr Merivale—Mother.

Merivale (*heartily*) Delighted to meet you. We shall be seeing
a good deal of each other, I've no doubt. You'll be coming round
tonight, of course?

Mrs Thursby. Tonight?

Merivale. You haven't told your own mother, Roger? (*He
crosses below Mrs Thursby to the door down* L) Dear, dear—these
young people. Well, now's your chance. I look forward to meeting

you again, Mrs Thursby—we shall have a great deal to discuss, a great deal.

(MERIVALE *exits down* L)

MRS THURSBY. What a funny man! What did he mean, Roger? What did you have to tell me?

ROGER (*crossing to* R *of the desk* R) Later, Mother. I'm not sure myself yet.

MRS THURSBY (*moving* C) I can't join you tonight, Roger, anyway. I'm going out with Mr Grimes.

ROGER. You're seeing an awful lot of each other these days.

MRS THURSBY. Do you disapprove?

ROGER. Of course not. It's time you enjoyed yourself.

MRS THURSBY. Thank you, darling. Why did I come in? I know—have you any money?

(ROGER *takes some coins from his pocket*)

ROGER. Ten shillings and sixpence ha'penny.

MRS THURSBY. Can I take the ten shillings?

ROGER. I can't buy lunch for sixpence ha'penny.

MRS THURSBY. We'll split it. I'll take seven and six. (*She takes some coins out of Roger's hand*)

ROGER. Split it? All right.

MRS THURSBY. I wish we had a little money, Roger.

ROGER (*moving above the desk* R) That's what we have—a little.

MRS THURSBY (*sitting* L *of the desk* R) Then I mean a lot. I'm so tired of scrimping and scraping. Will it be long before you get a really big case?

ROGER. I don't know. (*He suddenly leans towards her*) Would you be pleased, Mother, if I told you I had a chance to earn—well—say—three thousand pounds?

MRS THURSBY. Roger! It would be heaven.

(ROGER *puts his arms fondly around her*)

ROGER. It might be nearer than you think. You haven't thought of anyone but me for years. It's time I did something for you.

MRS THURSBY. I'm very lucky to have a son like you. Three thousand pounds!

ROGER. It isn't definite yet.

MRS THURSBY. But it will be. I knew you'd succeed—I knew it.

(*The sound of a taxi horn is heard off*)

(*She rises*) Oh, I must fly. The taxi's waiting—and if I don't hurry the seven and six won't be enough to pay the fare.

ROGER. You borrowed money to pay for a taxi!

MRS THURSBY. Of course. 'Bye, darling. (*She crosses to the*

door down L) Have a good time tonight wherever you're going.
'Bye.

(MRS THURSBY *blows a kiss to Roger and exits down* L. ROGER
*smiles, shakes his head, moves to his desk, picks up the brief and looks
at it*)

ROGER (*to himself*) Only once—faint and dizzy.

(SALLY *enters down* L. *She carries a file of papers*)

SALLY (*crossing to* C; *smiling*) Ah, all clear at last.
ROGER (*smiling*) Hello, Sally. (*He remembers*) Yes, it's all over.
SALLY (*moving to* R *of her desk* LC) You sound as though you've
been to a funeral. (*She puts her file on the desk*)
ROGER. It does feel rather like that. My own funeral.
SALLY. Did it go badly?
ROGER. Yes, it did—but that isn't it.
SALLY. Then what is the . . . ? Don't tell me! Our dinner date
is off.
ROGER (*crossing to Sally*) Sally . . .
SALLY (*angrily*) Keep away. (*She moves behind her desk*) What's
that woman got that I haven't—apart from an uncle who is a
successful solicitor?
ROGER. She's not in your class, Sally.
SALLY. But you're going to dinner with her tonight.
ROGER. I have to.
SALLY. Because uncle has promised you a nice juicy brief.
ROGER. No. I suppose—yes—in a way.
SALLY. There is a name for that sort of thing, you know—(*she
moves to* L *of the desk*) and not a pleasant one.
ROGER (*moving below the right end of the desk; angry because she is
right*) What does that remark mean?
SALLY. I should have thought it was quite clear.
ROGER. And I should have thought you would have been
pleased that I had the opportunity to get on.
SALLY (*moving up* L *of the desk*) I'm not complaining at your
getting on—it's the continual getting-off that bores me.
ROGER (*moving up* R *of the desk*) I'm glad I bore you.
SALLY. Yes, you do! Your pomposity bores me, your self-
righteousness bores me. (*Angrily, and mimicking his tone*) I've got
to be firm, Sally—the Bar is a whole-time job—I haven't time
for love. Oh, you—you hypocrite. You detestable, beastly hypocrite.

(*They face each other across the desk*)

ROGER (*equally angry*) If you had the chance of work—loads of
good briefs—would you turn them down?
SALLY (*leaning across the desk*) It depends what I was asked to
do in return. I wouldn't pay *that* price.

D

ROGER. I suppose it hasn't occurred to you that I might be getting the work on my own merits?

SALLY. No, it hasn't. Neither has it occurred to you—and you know it. Every brief that Merivale sends you is a sprat to catch a mackerel. (*With contempt*) Or rather, a mackerel to catch a sprat. (*She sits at her desk*)

ROGER (*moving* R) What I do is my own affair.

SALLY. Don't worry—I've no wish to interfere with your affairs. (*She takes her handbag from the desk drawer*) They're rather sordid for my taste. (*She slams the drawer shut*)

ROGER. You're damned insulting . . .

SALLY (*rising and standing* R *of her desk; interrupting*) Other people don't matter to you, Roger—not one little bit. They're just—just rungs on a ladder as far as you're concerned. You'd sell yourself like a—like a you-know-what—just to get on.

ROGER (*livid; quietly*) Have you quite finished?

SALLY. Yes, I've finished. Quite, quite finished, thank you.

(SALLY *looks at Roger and for a moment it seems as though she may soften.*
HENRY *enters breezily down* L. SALLY *sits at her desk*)

HENRY (*crossing to* C) Congratulations, congratulations, congratulations! Just met old Merivale in the Strand. He told me the glad news, old boy—(*he holds out his hand to Roger*) put it there.

(ROGER *ignores Henry's hand, his eyes still fixed angrily on Sally*)

SALLY. What news, Henry?

HENRY. Roger is engaged. To old Merivale's niece. Joy Watsername. He's like a dog with two tails. Don't wonder at it. I mean—aren't you going to shake, old boy?

(ROGER *turns his back to Henry*)

SALLY (*icily*) Congratulations, Roger. (*She collects her hat and coat from the hooks up* L *and puts them on*) Coming to lunch, Henry?

HENRY (*moving down* LC) Ready, my poppet.

SALLY (*moving down* L *of her desk*) Then let's go.

(ALEC *enters down* L, *carrying a brief*)

ALEC (*crossing to Henry*) Ah, there you are at last, Mr Blagrove. This brief was sent down for you this morning. (*He hands the brief to Henry*)

HENRY. A brief! Thank you, my dear Alec.

(ALEC *exits down* L)

Sally—no *Corner House* today—we'll lunch in style. (*He glances at the brief*) Mmm—a nice juicy divorce—Newent against Newent.

ROGER (*turning to Henry*) What was that?

HENRY. Newent against Newent.

ROGER (*eagerly*) I wanted to ask your advice about that, Henry. I'm really rather worried about it. You see, I'm appearing for Mrs Newent and . . .

HENRY. Sorry. Can't discuss it. I've just been briefed on the other side. For *Mr* Newent.*

(ROGER *is somewhat dazed.* HENRY *offers* SALLY *his arm. She takes it, goes to the door, pauses, then with great deliberation she crosses to Roger and kicks him on each shin.* ROGER *gives an agonized* "*ouch*" *at each blow*)

SALLY. I always keep *my* promises. (*She crosses to Henry*) Ready Henry?

(SALLY *and* HENRY *exit down* L. ROGER *hops from leg to leg as*—

the CURTAIN *falls*

* (*Alternative* CURTAIN)

ACT III

SCENE—*A Court Room and corridor at Bilborough Assizes. Ten days later.*

The corridor is represented by the downstage section of the stage with the court room beyond, the intervening wall being "cut away". The entrance to the corridor from the street is down R. Double doors up L leads to an ante-room and thence into the court. There is a window L with a bench under it, outside the double doors. In the court-room, in addition to the door from the ante-room L, there is a door R leading to the judge's room. The judge's bench and chair is on a rostrum R and in front of it is a chair and table for the clerk. The witness-box is up RC and L of it are benches for counsel. The dock, with a chair is L. We imagine that the audience is the jury, and the public seats are not in view.

When the CURTAIN *rises, the stage is in darkness. The lights come up on the corridor, leaving the court-room in darkness.* ROGER *rushes in down R. He is gowned and wigged and carries a file of papers. He looks about, then takes out a small mirror and looks at himself in it.* MRS THURSBY *enters down R.* ROGER *hastily conceals the mirror.*

ROGER. Mother, what on earth are you doing here?

MRS THURSBY. Darling, I *had* to come.

ROGER. Why?

MRS THURSBY. I've got something to do. I can't think what—but I know it's very important.

ROGER. Then you'd better go and do it, Mother. You shouldn't be here at all, really. I've got important things to do, too, you know.

MRS THURSBY. More examinations?

ROGER (*moving* C) Now, Mother, really! You know it can't be examinations. Not here. And you know very well I'm qualified.

MRS THURSBY. But you could still have examinations. Doctors do—and they're qualified. The one who helped me with you when you were born said he hoped to become a gynaecologist.

(GRIMES *bustles in down R. He pulls up short on seeing Mrs Thursby. There is something strangely nervous in his manner, strange for him.* MRS THURSBY *is very pleased to see him*)

GRIMES (*crossing and standing between Roger and Mrs Thursby*) Ah, you're here already, m'dear fellow—excellent—excellent. Amanda—I didn't expect—I didn't . . .

MRS THURSBY. Aren't you pleased to see me?

GRIMES (*recovering*) Of course. I was—er—just surprised m'dear. What brings you to Bilborough, eh? The regetta?

To face page 48— "*Brothers In Law*"

Photograph by Kenneth Simmons

MRS THURSBY. No, Kennie—it's something much more important. Only I can't remember what it is.

ROGER (*to Grimes*) I didn't know you were coming. Have you
got a case here?

GRIMES (*awkwardly*) Well—er—no—not exactly. I thought
I'd look in, just to see how things went, m'dear fellow. I've been
so busy—haven't really had time to talk to you properly.
Thought we might get an opportunity here—away from chambers, y'know.

ROGER. To talk? I mean—er—anything—I haven't done anything . . .

GRIMES. Of course not, m'dear fellow. No—what I had in
mind was—er—well, getting to know you and all that. Time we
discussed the future, eh? (*He gives a quick, embarrassed glance at
Mrs Thursby*)

(MRS THURSBY *smiles sweetly*)

ROGER. It's jolly decent of you to come all this way. I mean,
I know how busy you are.

GRIMES. We can do too much, y'know. Nose to the grindstone
too much—we can—er—overlook—er—other things in life, eh?
We will do these things, my boy, we will do 'em. (*To Mrs Thursby*)
Have you remembered what it is ye've come for, m'dear?

MRS THURSBY. Not yet. But it will come to me. It always does.
Shall I—er—leave you two men?

GRIMES. Mmm—yes—if ye don't mind, m'dear.

MRS THURSBY. I can always remember better when I'm walk-
ing. I'll take a little stroll. (*To Grimes. Softly*) Good luck.

(MRS THURSBY *blows Grimes a little kiss and exits down* R)

GRIMES (*a little heartily for him*) Quite a family party, eh?
Blagrove is against you in both cases, isn't he? Which is to be the
first.

ROGER. Green.

GRIMES. Ah, our friend Green. That should take care of itself.

ROGER. I feel rather nervous, I must admit.

GRIMES. Nothing to be nervous about, m'dear fellow. Nothing
at all. Just tell 'em the tale, tell 'em the tale.

ROGER. I'd better go and find Green, I think. (*He turns to go*)

GRIMES (*stopping Roger*) Don't ye worry, m'dear fellow. If he
doesn't come they'll find him for ye. But there was something . . .
Do sit down, m'dear fellow.

ROGER (*sitting on the bench*) Yes?

GRIMES (*awkwardly*) Well—I said I hadn't got a case here. I
have, as a matter of fact. Never done this sort of thing before.
Feel rather nervous.

ROGER. Nothing to be nervous about, m'dear . . . (*He checks
himself*) You feel nervous? About a case? Impossible.

GRIMES. Roger, my case is—I want to marry Amanda.

ROGER (*rising*) Congratulations! Wait—you mean mother?

GRIMES. That's it, exactly. Your mother.

ROGER. Oh.

GRIMES. You don't like the idea?

ROGER (*sitting on the bench*) It's a bit of a shock. How long has it . . . ? I mean . . .

GRIMES (*sitting beside Roger on the bench*) Years. I should have asked her ages ago. Glad I didn't, in a way.

ROGER. Why?

GRIMES. If I *had* asked her, she wouldn't have met your father. You might not have existed, d'you see?

ROGER. Yes, I do see. Or my name might have been Grimes. You might have been my father.

GRIMES. Never thought of that. Well, we will do these things— or not, as the case may be.

ROGER. And now you *do* want to be my father.

GRIMES. Er—mmm—yes. Though that isn't the chief object of the exercise, m'dear fellow. (*He rises and clears his throat*) Your mother is a wonderful woman, wonderful. She—er—insisted that I speak to you before she accepted my—er—proposal. She won't agree unless you do.

(*There is a long pause*)

ROGER (*not helping very much*) Yes?

GRIMES. Well, there it is, m'dear fellow. In a nutshell. I've a pretty good position at the Bar, as you know. I think I could keep her in the—er—way of life to which she's been accustomed.

ROGER. Better, I should hope. I've never been able to do much for her.

GRIMES. Then you agree?

ROGER (*rising; with a smile*) Of course. Nothing to do with me, really. I just want mother to be happy.

GRIMES. I'll do my utmost, m'dear fellow. (*He pumps Roger's hand*) Thank you, thank you, thank you.

ROGER (*glancing at his watch*) Heavens—look at the time. (*He crosses to* R) I must find Green. (*He stops and turns*) Er—I hope you'll both be—er—very happy.

GRIMES. No doubt of it, m'dear fellow, no doubt at all. (*He rubs his hands together with pleasure*) Well—that wasn't too bad for a first case, y'know, not too bad at all.

(GRIMES *chuckles to himself and exits by the double doors* L.
    GREEN *and* BRADLEY *enter down* R. ROGER *turns to go and almost collides with* GREEN)

GREEN. Oi, oi—careful—don't knock yourself out before you get started.

Roger. It's getting late. (*He moves* c)

Green. I'm never late. Guilty sometimes, yes. But as old Justice Thundersley once said—"You might be a rogue, Green", he said, "but you're punctual." On the dot, that's me. (*To Bradley*) Here, old son, you nip into court and find yourself a seat where you won't be noticed and you can read your comics in peace. (*To Roger*) He gets bored with court cases.

(Bradley *exits by the double doors up* l)

Now, Mr Thursby, you're all ready for the fray? No collywobbles, I hope?

Roger. A few. They say the judge can be difficult.

Green. What's a judge, anyway? Look at me—my teeth aren't chattering, are they?

Roger. No.

Green. I'm not shaking like a lily, am I?

Roger. No.

Green. Okay, then. Take a leaf out of my book. Anyone would think you was the prisoner and I was the counsel.

(Sally *and* Henry *enter down* r. *Both are wigged and gowned.* Henry *is slightly ahead of Sally. During the ensuing scene there is an awkwardness between* Roger *and* Sally; *an odd look passes between them*)

Henry. Sorry—I didn't realize . . . I'll just get . . .

Green. Don't go on my account, sir. I've got to get back to the royal suite myself.

Sally. Good morning, Mr Green.

Green. Ah, glad you're here, miss. I was hoping. You going to be in court?

Sally. Yes, I am.

Green. I like to have something to look at beside the judge.

Sally. I wouldn't miss your performance for the world, Mr Green.

Green. That's very nicely put. How do I look? Hair all right, miss?

Sally. Beautiful.

Green. Trouser creases?

Roger. Like razors.

Green. Took a lot of trouble over them.

Henry. I really ought not to be here—after all, I'm prosecuting.

Green. Don't apologize, sir. No ill feelings. Least said soonest mended. So long as you don't mind losing the case.

Henry. Thank you.

Green. It's a pity that two nice blokes like you can't both win.

SALLY. Forgive my mentioning it, but oughtn't you to have surrendered to your bail by now?

GREEN. I know me rights, miss. I don't surrender till they've called me names three times—once in the court—all nice and gentlemanly—(*in a fake cultured accent; quietly*) "Arthur Green, surrender." That's number one. Dear, dear! No Arthur Green. So the bloke at the door has his chance. (*In his ordinary voice, loudly*) "Arthur Green, surrender." That's number two. Dear, dear, dear, still no Arthur Green. So it's up to the bloke down the corridor. Last chance. (*Very loudly*) "Arthur Green, surrender." I wait for 'im.

USHER (*off; calling*) Arthur Green, surrender.

GREEN. Nice bit of timing. (*He pauses and straightens his tie*) Pity I flogged me gold tooth, though.

(GREEN *crosses and exits by the double doors up* L. ROGER *follows Green to* L)

SALLY (*crossing to Roger*) Roger . . .

ROGER (*eager to be friendly*) Yes, Sally?

SALLY. I—er—good luck.

HENRY. Same here. Best of luck.

ROGER. Thanks. Same to you. I mean—anyway, thanks.

(ROGER *gives a last look at Sally then exits by the double doors up* L. SALLY *sits on the bench*)

HENRY (*crossing to Sally*) He'll be all right. He's got Green on his side. Haven't heard much more about his engagement recently—is that still on?

SALLY. As far as I know. We haven't discussed it.

HENRY (*shivering*) Brrh—it's cold here. Lunch with me, Sally?

SALLY. If you like.

HENRY. I do, I do. Moreover, I have something to tell you. Of the very highest importance.

SALLY. You're not going to propose again? I'm not really in the mood.

HENRY. That is only part of it. (*He sits beside Sally on the bench*) I have decided to work.

SALLY. What?

HENRY. Aha—I knew that would throw you. The very idea terrifies me. I'll tell you at lunch.

(ALEC *enters by the double doors up* L)

ALEC. Better get in, sir.

HENRY (*rising*) Just going, Alec.

(SALLY *rises*)

ALEC (*offering his bag*) Toffee?

HENRY. I never touch it during the day, Alec. Later.

HENRY, SALLY *and* ALEC *exit by the double doors up* L *as—*

the LIGHTS BLACK-OUT

During the BLACK-OUT *there is music while the characters take their places in the court-room.*

When the LIGHTS *come up on the court-room, the case is about to start and the jury are about to be sworn.* MR JUSTICE KING *is seated on his bench. The* CLERK OF ASSIZE *is standing at his table, waiting to announce the names of the jury to the prisoner.* ROGER *is seated on counsel's bench at the right end.* SALLY *is standing* L *of Roger and* HENRY L *of Sally. On the bench behind counsel are* BRADLEY *and* ALEC. GREEN *is in the dock, with the* WARDER *beside him. The* USHER *stands up* L. *We see* BRADLEY *for a moment as he rises and peers at the dock.* GREEN *waves* BRADLEY *down and he resumes his seat, where he remains asleep until the end of the Act. The* JUDGE *notices this waving, looks at the barristers' benches, but* BRADLEY *is now out of sight.* GREEN *catches the* JUDGE'S *eye, pretends to brush his hair with his hand and grins.* SALLY *and* HENRY *bow to the Judge and sit.* ROGER *sees the bow, hastily rises, bows, drops his papers and makes quite a disturbance picking them up. He then peers into the audience. The* JUDGE *coughs menacingly at* ROGER, *who sits down anxiously and whispers to Sally.*

JUDGE. I've warned counsel once before about chattering.

(*The* CLERK *sits*)

ROGER (*rising*) My lord . . .
JUDGE (*snapping*) If you've got an application to make, you will kindly wait.
ROGER. But . . .
JUDGE. Will you please sit down.
ROGER. My lord, I want to mention . . .
JUDGE. If you don't know the rules, ask someone who does. I've told you once to wait.

(ROGER *sits, then rises again*)

ROGER (*desperately*) My lord, my lord . . .
JUDGE (*coldly*) I have been a judge now for a good many years, but I have never yet seen counsel behave in this shocking manner. Justice could not be administered—justice could not be administered, I say, unless all directions from the Bench were observed by the Bar. I have never known . . .

(ROGER, *defeated, sits*)

Thank you, thank you very much. (*He nods to the Clerk*)
CLERK (*rising*) Arthur Green, the names that you are about to hear called are the names of the jurors . . .

ROGER (*rising*) My lord, my lord—I want to . . .

(*The* CLERK *sits*)

JUDGE. I do not know your name, but that, in view of your extraordinary behaviour, I do not find surprising. Will you now do me the personal favour of resuming your seat?

ROGER. I want to draw your Lordship's attention . . .

JUDGE. You have already succeeded in doing that. Now—(*he almost shouts*) if you do not sit down, I shall be under the painful duty of reporting you to your Benchers.

ROGER. Please, my lord . . .

JUDGE (*thundering*) I order you to sit down!

(ROGER *sits*)

ROGER (*after a brief pause*) I object to the juror in the hat. She is my mother.

(*There is a pause in which all scrutinize the audience*)

GREEN. *I* don't object, my lord. I like the look of her.

(ROGER *wipes his brow*)

JUDGE (*to Green*) You be quiet! (*He whispers to the Clerk and nods*) Mr Thursby.

SALLY. Get up, Roger—he's going to apologize.

(ROGER *rises*)

JUDGE. Mr Thursby—I owe you a very humble apology. I am extremely sorry. By my haste, I have placed you in a position which would have been horribly embarrassing for any member of the Bar and which—for one of—if I may say so without offence—your limited experience must have been almost beyond bearing. You dealt with the situation with a courage and a patience which I shall long remember.

ROGER (*indistinctly*) Thank you, my lord. (*He sits*)

JUDGE (*looking over the audience*) You had better leave the jury-box, madam.

CLERK (*rising*) Will you come this way, madam? (*He sits*)

(MRS THURSBY *enters down* R *and moves up* C)

JUDGE (*to Mrs Thursby*) I owe you an apology, too, and I should like to say that you have every reason for being proud of your son.

MRS THURSBY (*smiling*) Thank you.

GREEN. I would like to say, my lord, that I'm proud of him, too. Picked him out myself—almost threw him back—but you should have seen the one that got away.

JUDGE. Be quiet.

(Mrs Thursby *pats Roger, crosses and exits up* LC)

Clerk (*rising*) Arthur Green, the names that you are about to hear called are the names of the jurors who are to pass between our Sovereign Lady the Queen and the prisoner at the bar . . .

The lights dim to Black-Out *for a few moments to denote a slight passage of time.*

When the Lights *come up, the Green case is in progress.* Green *is standing in the witness-box.* Roger *is standing, examining Green. The* Clerk *has resumed his seat. The* Usher *is standing* L *of the witness-box.*

Roger. Have you ever cheated anyone before?
Green. Steady!
Judge. Behave yourself. Your case is being conducted admirably by Mr Thursby. Perhaps, though, that last question might be re-phrased.
Green. Beg pardon, my lord. I get carried away by my natural exuberance.
Judge. Control it—or I may be carried away by mine. Continue, Mr Thursby.
Roger. Mr Green—who wrote the reference which was sent to Mr Digby?
Green. I did. But that's not important—what's important is *when* I sent it. Ask me that.
Judge. I shan't . . .
Green. Very sorry, my lord.
Roger. When did you send the reference to Mr Digby?
Green. On the ninth of July.
Roger (*taking the receipt from his papers*) Do you identify this receipt for posting? (*He hands the receipt to Green*)

(*The* Judge *coughs. The* Usher *snatches the receipt from Green and returns it to Roger.* Roger *formally hands the receipt to the* Usher *who hands it to Green*)

Green (*looking at the receipt*) I do.

(*The* Usher *takes the receipt from Green, passes it to the Judge, then returns to* L *of the witness-box.* Roger *sits*)

(*To Roger. Sotto voce*) Not bad—not bad at all.

(Henry *rises to cross-examine Green*)

Henry. Now, Mr Green—do I rightly understand your evidence to be this? You offered to supply toffee to Mr Digby, and offered to send him a reference. He does not wait for the reference, but sends the money.
Green. That's right. He was impatient to get his teeth into it—the toffee, I mean.

HENRY. Kindly wait until I have finished. After you received the money from Mr Digby, you sent him a reference which you had written yourself but which is signed in a false name. Is that your story?

GREEN. That is not only my story, but it happens to be true. I hope you don't mind.

JUDGE. Don't be impertinent.

GREEN. I don't intend to be impertinent, my lord, but I have a little way of talking sometimes which makes people think I do. Perhaps I'd better apologize in advance.

JUDGE. Be quiet! You're not doing yourself any good by making these silly speeches.

HENRY. Did the customer get less toffee than he had paid for?

GREEN. That's possible. I had a very bad man doing the packing at the time. He made away with a lot of toffee.

HENRY. Who was this man?

GREEN. Well—the name he gave me was "Brown"—without an "e"—but of course it might have been a false name—you've no idea of the rogues you can find in the toffee business.

HENRY. Did you ever get a reference for him?

GREEN (*looking at the Judge's table*) I don't much care for references.

HENRY. Are you sure there ever *was* a Mr Brown—without an "e"?

GREEN. Of course. I can describe him.

HENRY. Please do.

(GREEN *describes the player taking the part of* HENRY, *the following details being altered to fit*)

GREEN. Aged about thirty-five, middling height, brown hair, small moustache—slight paunch—funny way of standing with his hands on his hips.

(HENRY *reacts*)

Of course, he might have shaved off the moustache by now. Fond of toffee, he was.

JUDGE (*after a pause*) Any more questions, Mr Blagrove?

HENRY (*to Green*) I suggest that you sent the reference before you received the money.

(GREEN *points to the Judge's table. The* JUDGE *fumbles for the receipt, finds it and* GREEN *nods*)

Will you answer my question?

JUDGE. Well, Mr Blagrove, it's a pretty good answer, isn't it? This is certainly a genuine document, anyway. I can't, of course, say there's no evidence, but it may be that the jury will say they have heard enough already.

HENRY. My lord, the question of attempting to obtain money by false pretences could arise.

GREEN. How can it? How can I attempt to obtain money which I've already received?

JUDGE. Exactly. (*He reacts*) Mr Green—I have repeatedly warned you . . .

GREEN. Sorry, my lord—very sorry. Just at this stage I kind of get excited.

JUDGE. Will you be quiet.

(HENRY *sits*)

(*He looks towards the audience*) Members of the jury, fortunately for the prisoner he is not charged with talking too much—indeed, if there were such an offence, some of us might find our way into the dock. Even I . . .

GREEN (*cheekily*) Never.

(*The* JUDGE *reacts*)

JUDGE. How dare you!

GREEN. I was only standing up for you, my lord.

JUDGE. Mr Thursby——

(ROGER *rises*)

—will you kindly see that your client behaves.

(ROGER *has no idea what to do. He looks around the court, fumbles with his papers, looks towards Green, mouths at him and resumes his seat.* GREEN *nods approvingly at Roger*)

Thank you, Mr Thursby.

ROGER (*rising quickly*) If your lordship pleases. (*He sits*)

JUDGE. That's all right, Mr Thursby.

ROGER (*rising quickly*) Thank you, my lord. (*He sits*)

JUDGE. Very well, then.

(ROGER *starts to rise*)

(*He waves Roger down. To the audience*) Members of the jury, there is only one charge against the prisoner, and whatever you may think about his antics, his guilt has to be established. Perhaps you'd like to have a word with one another.

GREEN (*to Roger; rubbing his hands*) It's in the bag.

JUDGE (*angrily*) One more word—one more word and I shall send you to prison for contempt of court. I shall adjourn for lunch now.

GREEN. My lord . . .

JUDGE. Perhaps during the adjournment the jury will consider what I have said.

GREEN. My lord . . .

JUDGE (*rising*) One more word . . .

GREEN. I only wanted to know if it was all right for me to speak during lunch.

The LIGHTS BLACK-OUT.
During the BLACK-OUT, *all exit from the court-room.*
The LIGHTS *come up on the corridor.* MERIVALE, JOY *and* MRS NEWENT *enter down* R. JOY *crosses to* L.

MRS NEWENT (*moving* C) All I can say is, I hope you're right, that's all. I hope he's old enough to know what he's doing. I never thought the old basket would go on defending . . .

MERIVALE (*moving* R *of Mrs Newent*) We have every confidence in Mr Thursby.

MRS NEWENT. I dare say. It's this discretion business that worries me. If I'd had my way, I would have kept quiet about it. After all—it is my business.

MERIVALE. Hm—hm—we have a duty to the court, you know.

MRS NEWENT. Fiddle-faddle! A lot of old fools sitting up there. What do they know?

MERIVALE. More than you think. For one thing, most of them were young fools once.

JOY. People who know say that Roger—Mr Thursby—has a brilliant future at the Bar.

MRS NEWENT. I hope they know what they're talking about. I want this divorce.

(ROGER *enters hurriedly by the double doors up* L)

JOY (*moving to* L *of Roger*) Oh, Roger—darling—you look wonderful.

MRS NEWENT (*sarcastically*) That's the way the wind blows, is it? Someone wants their brains tested.

(SALLY *enters by the double doors up* L)

MERIVALE. How did it go, my boy?

ROGER (*modestly*) Rather well, actually. Jury threw out the case.

JOY. That's wonderful! You see, Uncle, I told you.

ROGER. It was luck, really.

MRS NEWENT (*to Sally*) Was he all right?

SALLY. He did very well.

MRS NEWENT. Well, he'd better do very well again.

(MRS NEWENT *minces out by the double doors up* L)

MERIVALE. I'd better see her safely in. (*He moves to the double doors*) Afterwards, perhaps we can have lunch, my boy. I'm—er—rather surprised that you haven't given me an answer on that other matter. We can't wait indefinitely, you know.

(MERIVALE *exits by the double doors up* L)

JOY (*with a glance at Sally*) Could we have a moment alone, Roger, do you think?

ROGER. I ought to go into court.

SALLY. So sorry—am I in the way?

ROGER. No—not at all. I really must go—excuse me, Joy.

(ROGER *exits hurriedly by the double doors up* L)

JOY (*sitting on the bench*) Well!

SALLY. I shouldn't worry. Roger has a great deal on his mind, you know.

JOY. I hope it isn't going to be like this always. Do you know I've hardly seen him this past week or two? Always some excuse or other about work.

SALLY (*pleased*) Really?

JOY. You know we're engaged, of course.

SALLY. I had heard.

JOY. And you heard what my uncle just said. It doesn't matter your knowing—it will come out sooner or later. Uncle has offered him the most marvellous brief, and he just won't give a direct answer.

SALLY. Good for Roger. (*She moves* LC *and turns to Joy*) I mean—you surprise me.

JOY. Uncle is getting very impatient.

SALLY. Understandably.

JOY (*rising*) He thinks a great deal of you.

SALLY. Your uncle?

JOY. No—Roger.

SALLY (*turning away* C) Did he tell you that?

JOY. He's always speaking of you. Er—I mean—in relation to work, of course. He admires your judgement. If you could advise him—I mean—the right word in the right place . . . I'm only thinking of his career.

SALLY (*moving to the double doors*) I'll most certainly see what I can do.

JOY (*smiling*) Thank you. Are you going in?

SALLY. Oh, yes.

JOY (*moving to the double doors*) I'll come with you. You know when I first saw you—I'll admit it—I didn't really understand you. That's all over. We are friends? After all, we both want Roger to be happy, don't we?

SALLY. Exactly. That's just the way I should put it. (*She stands aside*) After you.

JOY. Oh, no—after you.

SALLY. Thank you.

(ALEC *enters hurriedly by the double doors*)

ALEC. I don't like it, I don't like it. (*He sits on the bench*)

SALLY. Has something gone wrong?

ALEC. Mr Commissioner Crane has been taken ill. He can't hear Newent and Newent.

JOY. But what's the matter?

ALEC. Mr Justice King is going to hear it as a special favour—a special favour, I ask you. I don't believe he's ever done a divorce case in his life. And he's a bachelor.

JOY. Roger'll be all right. I've a great opinion of him.

ALEC (rising) Well, I hope Mrs Newent is going to have one, too, when it's all over.

JOY. I'm sure you don't have to worry. Roger's got all his speech prepared. He read it out to me.

ALEC (after a sigh) And Mrs Newent and Mr Merivale will have their speeches all prepared when we've lost the case.

JOY (moving C) Now, that's where I can help. Mr Merivale has the highest opinion of Roger—and I'm going to see that he doesn't change it.

ALEC (grimly) Pity you're not doing the case, miss.

(ALEC exits by the double doors up L)

JOY. Well, really, what a fuss. You think Roger will be all right, don't you?

SALLY. I hope so, but I'm afraid I haven't Mr Green's confidence.

JOY. But he got off.

SALLY. Mr Green did. I hope Roger will. Come and sit in court with me.

JOY. Right. (She moves to the double doors)

SALLY. After you.

JOY. No, after you.

(MRS THURSBY enters by the double doors and crosses to C.
SALLY and JOY exit by the double doors.
GRIMES enters down R)

MRS THURSBY. Kennie!

GRIMES (crossing to C) Amanda—I've been looking for you.

MRS THURSBY. What did he say?

GRIMES. He took it very well.

MRS THURSBY. He gave his consent?

GRIMES. Officially.

MRS THURSBY. Oh, Kennie!

(They exchange a light kiss)

Did you tell him the tale?

The LIGHTS BLACK-OUT.
During the BLACK-OUT, MRS THURSBY and GRIMES exit. The LIGHTS come up on the court-room. The JUDGE is not yet sitting. MERIVALE is seated on the bench behind counsel. MRS NEWENT

is seated L *of Merivale.* ROGER *is seated at the right end of the down-stage bench.* HENRY *and the* CLERK *are standing* C, *talking.*

HENRY. The old boy's determined to try the case, but he'll pretend he doesn't want to.
ROGER. What do I do?
HENRY. Leave it to me.
ROGER. Thanks very much.

(*There are three loud knocks off* R. MERIVALE, ROGER *and* MRS NEWENT *rise.*
    The USHER *enters up* R)

USHER. Silence in court.

(*The* JUDGE *enters up* R, *moves to his seat and bows. Everyone in the court bows. The* USHER *seats the Judge, then moves and stands up* R. MERIVALE, ROGER *and* MRS NEWENT *resume their seats.* HENRY *sits* L *of Roger. The* CLERK *whispers to the Judge then sits at his table*)

JUDGE. Mr—ah—Thursby, I gather you want to apply to have a divorce case tried by me. It's most inconvenient.
ROGER (*rising*) My lord—my lord . . . (*He looks appealingly at Henry*)

(HENRY *rises and motions Roger to sit.* ROGER *resumes his seat*)

HENRY. If I can help your lordship. Mr Commissioner Crane has unfortunately been taken ill, and my client, Mr Newent, is a member of a crew of an air liner which takes off tomorrow. If your lordship could see your way to take it I should be most grateful.
JUDGE. How long will the case take?
HENRY. I can assure your lordship that it's a short case.
JUDGE. What does Mr Thursby say to that? D'you agree that it's a short case?
ROGER (*rising*) Oh, yes, my lord.
JUDGE (*grudgingly*) Very well, then, in all the circumstances, I'll take it.
HENRY. I'm most obliged, my lord. (*He sits*)

(ROGER *is standing, not knowing quite what to do*)

ROGER. May it please your lordship . . .
JUDGE. The case hasn't been called on yet, Mr Thursby.
ROGER. Oh, no, my lord. I'm sorry, my lord. (*He sits*)
CLERK. Newent against Newent.

(ROGER *is wondering whether he should rise*)

JUDGE. The case *has* been called on now, Mr Thursby.

E

ROGER (*jumping up and dropping his papers on the floor*) I'm sorry, my lord. I appear in this case . . .

JUDGE. Mr Thursby, I gather this is a wife's petition on the ground of desertion, and it's a discretion case?

ROGER. Yes, my lord.

JUDGE. Well, you don't want to open it, do you? Just call your client. D'you put in the discretion statement?

ROGER. Well—I . . . (*He looks appealingly at Henry*)

(HENRY *nods*)

Yes, my lord.

JUDGE. Very well, then. Let me see it.

(*The* CLERK *unseals an envelope and hands the discretion statement to the Judge*)

(*He reads the statement*) Go on with the evidence, Mr Thursby. I can listen and read at the same time.

ROGER. If your lordship pleases. Go into the witness-box, please, Mrs Newent.

(MRS NEWENT *rises and goes into the witness-box. The* CLERK *rises, hands a Bible to Mrs Newent and holds a printed card in front of her*)

CLERK. Take the book in your right hand and repeat the words on the card.

MRS NEWENT. I swear by the Almighty God . . .

CLERK. No, madam.

MRS NEWENT (*puzzled*) I swear by the Almighty God . . .

CLERK. No, madam. Read the words correctly.

MRS NEWENT (*still puzzled; slowly*) I swear by the Almighty God . . .

CLERK (*with a sigh*) Repeat the words after me, please, madam. I swear——

MRS NEWENT. I swear——

CLERK. —by Almighty God . . .

MRS NEWENT. —by the Almighty God . . .

CLERK. No, madam. "By Almighty God."

MRS NEWENT. That's what I said.

CLERK. You did not, madam. You said, "*the* Almighty God".

MRS NEWENT. Goodness gracious, what's the difference?

JUDGE (*looking up*) Behave yourself, madam, and take the oath properly.

MRS NEWENT. I swear by Almighty God that the evidence I shall give shall be the truth, the whole truth and nothing but the truth.

(*The* CLERK *takes the Bible and sits at his table. The* JUDGE *continues to read the statement*)

JUDGE (*without looking up*) Go on, Mr Thursby, I was told this was a short case.

ROGER. Is your full name Ethel Newent?

MRS NEWENT. Yes.

ROGER. And do you live at The Limes, Broad Oak Avenue, Merton?

JUDGE. Mr Thursby, you mustn't lead as to the address. I warned you that I could read and listen at the same time.

ROGER. I'm sorry, my lord. Er—er . . .

HENRY (*whispering*) Ask her where she lives.

ROGER. Where do you live?

MRS NEWENT. Thirteen, Portslade Road, Moreworth.

JUDGE. There you are, Mr Thursby. That shows the reason for the rule.

ROGER. Yes, my lord. Mrs Newent, were you married on the thirteenth of June, nineteen-forty-eight, at the Yiewsley Register Office, to the respondent, Kenneth Robert Newent?

MRS NEWENT. Yes.

ROGER. How did your married life go, Mrs Newent?

MRS NEWENT. At first it was lovely—(*confidentially*) you know, my lord, lovely . . .

JUDGE. I do *not* know, and please don't speak confidentially to me.

MRS NEWENT. Well—once he was used to me—he wasn't interested. You know—I mean, you don't know, my lord.

JUDGE. Not interested in what?

MRS NEWENT (*starting loudly, but finding it too difficult*) Well, my lord, to put it plainly—well—er . . .

JUDGE. Really! When I said I'd take this case I didn't know there'd be all this bother about it. Well, madam—I'm waiting for your answer.

MRS NEWENT. Er—yes, my lord.

JUDGE. It's perfectly simple. You've told me that at first every-thing was—to use your own word—lovely: that means, I suppose, that you went out together—went to cinemas, and theatres, went for outings—tennis, swimming and so on—all the usual things that a happily married couple do together?

MRS NEWENT. Yes, my lord.

JUDGE. And after a time he ceased to be interested?

MRS NEWENT. Yes, my lord.

JUDGE. And I said—in what?

MRS NEWENT. Yes, my lord.

JUDGE. Don't keep on saying—"Yes, my lord". Was it in tennis, bathing, cinemas, theatres . . . Oh—I see. Next question, Mr Thursby.

ROGER. And what happened in the end?

MRS NEWENT. He left me.

JUDGE. Let's get on, Mr Thursby. (*To Mrs Newent*) Has your husband ever offered to return to you, or make a home for you?

Mrs Newent. Oh, no, my lord.

Roger. Thank you, my lord.

Judge (*angry for a moment*) Is that remark intended to be humorous?

Roger. Oh, no, my lord. I was just—thanking your lordship—for—asking—my question.

Judge (*genially*) You have another one, I expect—Mr Thursby.

Roger. Well—er—no, my lord. (*He sits*)

Judge. What about discretion, Mr Thursby?

Roger (*rising quickly*) Oh! Of course—thank you, my lord—I mean . . .

Judge. That's all right, Mr Thursby, don't upset yourself. Take it quite slowly. There's plenty of time. (*He looks at the court clock and confirms it with his watch*)

Roger. Mrs Newent—will you look at your discretion statement?

(*The* Judge *hands the statement to the* Usher *who hands it to Mrs Newent*)

Is what you say there true, and is it the whole truth?

Mrs Newent. I suppose so.

Judge. What d'you mean—you *suppose* so?

Mrs Newent. Well, I wouldn't have signed it otherwise, would I, my lord?

Judge. I hope not—but there are people who sign documents which do not contain the truth.

Mrs Newent. Oh, dear.

(*The* Judge *looks at Mrs Newent to see if she is being impertinent, but decides that she is not intending to be*)

Judge. And what you've said is true?

Mrs Newent. Oh, yes, my lord.

Judge. Then you only misbehaved once with the man in question?

Mrs Newent. Yes, my lord—only once.

Judge. And did he ask you to do so again?

Mrs Newent (*virtuously and quickly*) Oh, no, my lord.

Judge. Why not?

Mrs Newent (*taken aback*) I beg your pardon, my lord?

Judge. Why not?

Mrs Newent (*musingly*) Yes—that *is* a question.

Judge. Well—what's the answer?

Mrs Newent. It's very odd—really it is.

Judge. It is indeed. I can understand your refusing, but I don't understand why he didn't ask.

Mrs Newent. Thank you, my lord.

JUDGE. Yes, Mr Thursby—your next question?

ROGER. Did your husband ever know about your misconduct?

MRS NEWENT. Oh—no—we were most careful about that.

JUDGE. Oh, you were, were you?

MRS NEWENT. Well—it seemed—better, my lord—that way, if you follow me.

JUDGE. Don't you think it would have been better to have confessed and asked for forgiveness?

MRS NEWENT. But he mightn't have forgiven me, my lord. And then where should I have been?

JUDGE. Any further questions?

ROGER. No, my lord. (*He sits*)

JUDGE. Very well, then. Yes, Mr Blagrove?

HENRY (*rising*) No questions, my lord. (*He sits*)

ROGER (*rising*) Thank you, Mrs Newent.

(*The* USHER *helps* MRS NEWENT *from the witness-box. She bobs to the Judge then resumes her seat on the upstage bench*)

JUDGE. Is that your case Mr Thursby?

ROGER. Er—yes my lord. (*He sits*)

JUDGE. Yes, Mr Blagrove?

HENRY (*rising*) I call no evidence, my lord. (*He sits*)

(*Nothing happens for a moment and* ROGER *does not know what the next move is*)

JUDGE. Mr Thursby, d'you want to say anything?

ROGER (*rising*) Well—er—my lord, doesn't Mr Blagrove . . . ?

JUDGE. No, Mr Thursby, as Mr Blagrove is calling no evidence, you come first.

(ROGER *fumbles with his papers*)

I think I see why Mr Blagrove is calling no evidence. I expect you do, too, Mr Thursby.

ROGER. Er—well, my lord . . .

JUDGE. It's pretty obvious, isn't it?

ROGER. Well, my lord, I—er . . . (*He looks hopelessly around*)

JUDGE. Shall I tell you what I think he's going to say?

ROGER (*sitting*) Thank you, my lord.

JUDGE. He is going to submit that as the petitioner committed adultery one week before her husband left her, she hasn't proved that the adultery did not cause the desertion.

ROGER (*rising slightly*) I see, my lord.

JUDGE. It seems to be a pretty good point, doesn't it? How d'you get out of it?

ROGER (*rising*) Well, my lord, I—er—Mrs Newent—my lord . . .

JUDGE. I suppose you rely on Herod and Herod?

Roger. Yes, my lord.

Judge. And you say that, strange as it may seem to many people, the law there laid down says that a husband or wife may commit adultery as much as he or she likes provided they're good enough liars to prevent the other spouse from finding out.

Roger. Yes, my lord.

Judge. And you say, I suppose, that your client *was* a good enough liar?

Roger. Er—(*he looks uncomfortably round at Mrs Newent; in a whisper*) Yes, my lord.

Judge. But that won't do, will it, Mr Thursby?

Roger. Won't do, my lord?

Judge. Won't do, Mr Thursby, will it?

Roger. I suppose not, my lord.

Judge. Then do you submit to having the petition dismissed, Mr Thursby?

Roger (*in dismay*) Dismissed, my lord?

Judge. Well, that's what it comes to, doesn't it? (*Friendly and confidingly*) You see, Mr Thursby, Herod says that the petitioner has to prove that her adultery did not cause the desertion. That's right, isn't it?

Roger. Yes, my lord.

Judge. Well, isn't it likely that the demeanour of a guilty wife may consciously or unconsciously cause her husband to leave her? Particularly as the adultery took place only a few days before the desertion. In such circumstances, how can you say that her conduct did not cause the desertion?

Roger. Well—the husband didn't know, my lord.

Judge (*a little startled that Roger has found his voice*) What's that? The husband didn't know, eh? But I have just explained why that need make no difference. Do you wish to add anything, Mr Thursby?

Roger. Er—er . . .

(*There is a pause*)

Merivale (*in a loud whisper*) Go on, say something, say something.

(*But poor* Roger *can only wave his hands and resume his seat*)

(*He rises*) My lord, I am the solicitor in this case—will your lordship allow me . . . ?

Judge (*sternly*) No, I will not allow you. I can neither hear you nor see you.

Merivale. But, my lord . . .

Judge. Be quiet, sir! Mr Thursby is saying—or has already said—all that can be said on behalf of the petitioner.

(Merivale *sits*)

Well, Mr Thursby, anything else you wish to add to your elo-
quent—mmm—ah—submission?

ROGER (*rising*) Er—er—I don't think so, my lord—no, my
lord. (*He sits with relief*)

JUDGE. Very well, then. For the reasons I have stated, the
petition will be dismissed. I take it, Mr Blagrove, that in the
circumstances, you do not ask for costs?

HENRY (*rising*) No, my lord. (*He sits*)

JUDGE. You wouldn't have got them.

(*The* JUDGE *rises. All in the court rise. The* JUDGE *bows. All in
the Court bow.*

The JUDGE, *assisted by the* USHER, *exits up* R. *The* USHER
follows him off. The CLERK *commences to speak as the Judge goes*)

CLERK. All persons having any further to do before my Lords
the Queen's Justices may now depart hence and give their
attendance at my lord's lodgings.

(MRS NEWENT *complains to Merivale.*
The CLERK *collects his papers, crosses and exits up* L)

HENRY (*to Roger*) Bad luck, old man. You will excuse me.

(HENRY *exits up* L)

MRS NEWENT. Well! (*She moves* C)

ROGER. I'm extremely sorry, Mrs Newent.

MRS NEWENT. Not half as sorry as I am. Cost me a pretty penny
and what have I got for it?

(MERIVALE *moves and stands* RC)

ROGER. I'm extremely sorry . . .

MRS NEWENT. You already said that, and it doesn't help.

(GRIMES *enters up* L)

I'm the one who's married to that So-and-so, not you.

MERIVALE. I've never heard such a deplorable performance in
all my life—never.

GRIMES (*crossing to Merivale*) He did his best, my dear fellow.
He's only just out of the egg.

MERIVALE. Pity he didn't stay in it.

GRIMES (*to Mrs Newent*) Don't you worry, my dear lady—it will
be all right.

MRS NEWENT. How will it be all right?

GRIMES. You can appeal, of course.

MERIVALE. Yes, I suppose the Court of Appeal might take a
different view—if the case is differently put.

MRS NEWENT. And I suppose it will cost me a packet. If you
ask me, it's all come about by employing schoolboys to do my
case.

GRIMES. Come, come—we were all young once, madam.

MRS NEWENT. Thank you! I might have expected you to stick
up for him. You would. But if you want my opinion, you're all a
bloody lot of twisters, and that's straight. Good afternoon. (*She
turns and sweeps to the door up* L)

(JOY *enters up* L *and practically collides with* MRS NEWENT)

Excuse me!

(MRS NEWENT *slams out up* L. JOY *moves to* ROGER *and leads
him* C)

JOY (L *of Roger*) I think Roger did very well in the circumstances, don't you, Uncle?

MERIVALE. No, I do not.

JOY. Oh, Uncle!

MERIVALE (*steadying himself*) Well, the judge *was* difficult.

GRIMES. Exactly so, m'dear fellow. Exactly so. Court of Appeal
will never wear that one. Dear me, no. Don't ye worry.

MERIVALE. You're sure of that?

GRIMES. Of course, m'dear fellow, of course.

(ALEC *enters up* L)

ALEC (*to Grimes*) Telephone for you, sir—London.

GRIMES. Just coming, Alec. (*He crosses to the door up* L) They
will do these things, they will do them. But that's what the
Court of Appeal's for—to put 'em right when they do them, my
dear fellow, to put 'em right.

(GRIMES *exits up* L)

ALEC (*to Roger*) Hard lines, sir. The judge was a b-bit of a
handful.

(ALEC *exits up* L. *There is a pause*)

ROGER (*to Merivale*) I am sorry, sir.

MERIVALE. Too late for that now. Well, we'll have to see that
the appeal is handled properly, that's all.

ROGER. You mean—you'll take me off the case?

JOY. You can't do that, Uncle.

MERIVALE (*tactfully*) This is a case where two heads will be
better than one. We'll take in a leader. (*He moves down* RC)

ROGER (*taking a deep breath*) Mr Merivale, I think I'd better
withdraw from the case altogether.

MERIVALE (*turning*) I beg your pardon. What did he say?

ROGER. I said—I will withdraw. (*With growing confidence*)
Furthermore, I have thought over your other offer—and with
respect—I must decline it.

JOY. Roger—have you gone mad?

ROGER. I've just come to my senses, Joy. Shall I tell you something? Something happened to me just now.

MERIVALE. You lost a perfectly good case.

ROGER. I know. But I'm not going to lose any more for some time—for the simple reason that I'm not going to do any more for some time.

JOY. What do you mean, Roger?

ROGER. I don't want to appear ungrateful or rude, but—the fact is—it isn't fair to the public to be represented by people like me who don't know how the job's done.

JOY. Have you gone out of your senses? Here's uncle and me trying to help you for all we're worth, and you throw it back in our teeth.

ROGER. I'm sorry, Joy—but I've just got things straight. I've got to see other barristers at work for at least a year before I'll feel ready to take a case of my own.

MERIVALE. Well, young man, I believe you've got something there.

JOY. Uncle—really—you're not helping.

ROGER. I'm sorry, Joy. I've treated you badly.

JOY. It'll be a long time before I try to help anyone again. (*She removes her engagement ring*) Here's your ring—oh—no, I forgot, it's mine.

(JOY *exits up* L)

MERIVALE. Well, my boy, if you stick to your guns, you'll do well. But there'll be temptations, mind you.

ROGER. Temptations?

MERIVALE. Yes. At any moment your clerk or someone will come along and ask you to do a case for someone else—or part of a case, even. What are you going to say then?

(SALLY *enters up* L)

SALLY. Am I in the way?

MERIVALE. Not at all. I was just going. Well, good luck, young man. There'll be another brief from Thornton, Merivale coming down to you one of these d— years.

(MERIVALE *crosses and exits up* L)

ROGER (*moving up* R *of the Clerk's table*) Phew!

SALLY (*moving down* L *of the Clerk's table*) What has been happening? Joy nearly knocked me down, she was running so fast.

ROGER (*perching on the Clerk's table; ruefully*) The blood rushed to my head—and out it all came. It's happened to me before. Every now and then—blood rushes to my head—and I just have to do something. This time I chucked the case, the uncle and the girl.

SALLY. Phew!

ROGER (*rising and moving to* R *of Sally*) I can feel it rushing up again. (*He takes Sally in his arms*) Sally—when you look at me like that I'm lost. (*He kisses her*)

> (SALLY *responds*.
> GRIMES *enters up* L, *carrying a brief*. SALLY *and* ROGER *break*)

GRIMES (*crossing to Roger*) My dear fellow—so sorry to interrupt you—you can just catch it.

ROGER. Catch it?

GRIMES. The train, m'dear fellow. I want ye to go to Manchester for me.

ROGER. Manchester?

SALLY. Manchester?

GRIMES. It's only a plea of guilty, but it'll be good practice for ye.

ROGER. But I'd just made up my mind not to appear in court until I've had more experience.

GRIMES. You're quite right, my dear fellow—absolutely right—ye oughtn't to appear in any case—except just this little plea of guilty in Manchester. You won't come to any harm.

ROGER. I'm thinking of the poor client. And besides, I wanted to take Sally out to tea—and dinner.

GRIMES. Well, which is it, my dear fellow? Is it picnics ye want or experience of standing up in court?

ROGER. Well, of course, I want to get on . . .

GRIMES (*leading Roger to the door up* L) So ye will, my dear fellow, if ye catch that train. There might be a seat in chambers for ye later.

ROGER. D'you mean that?

GRIMES. If ye leave out the picnics. For a while, at any rate.

ROGER. What's the case about?

GRIMES. Just a simple little case of obstruction by a motor car.

ROGER. But—d'you mean to say they're paying a barrister to go all the way to Manchester and plead guilty on a case like that? It'd be better to pay the fine and be done with it.

GRIMES. That depends whose car it is.

ROGER. And whose was it?

GRIMES. Mine, m'dear fellow. Good practice for ye—off ye go.

ROGER. What's the maximum fine?

GRIMES. Ye'll find out, my dear fellow, ye'll find out.

ROGER. Well . . .

GRIMES. Now, come on, my dear fellow. Here's the brief. Ye'll find all about it in there. Just don't let them send me to jail, that's all I ask.

ROGER. But they can't for obstruction.

GRIMES. D'ye think I'd have sent ye if they could?

ROGER. Good-bye, Sally. I'm sorry—you do understand? I—oh—I quite forgot. (*To Grimes*) What about mother?

GRIMES. I'm looking after mother. If ye do well in Manchester, they'll pay your fare home. (*He takes some notes from his wallet*) But just in case they don't . . . (*He hands the notes to Roger*)

ROGER. Oh—thanks. 'Bye, Sally. (*With a smile*) 'Bye, Father.

(ROGER *exits up* L)

GRIMES (*crossing to Sally*) That's jumping the gun a bit. (*He puts his arm around Sally and seats her in the Clerk's chair*) Still, I wouldn't call it a false start. Now, cheer up, my dear girl. It's not the end of the world, you know, only Manchester.

SALLY (*tearfully*) I know.

GRIMES (*paternally*) Ye wanted to take him over the hills and far away—before he'd learned to cross the road.

(HENRY *enters up* L *and crosses to* C)

Won't do, y'know, not at twenty-four. But there are chaps, my dear girl—(*he pats Henry on the back*) naming no names—there are chaps who'd do better for being married and having someone to work for.

HENRY. Oh—sorry—am I in the way?

GRIMES (*crossing to the door up* L) We shall see, m'dear fellow, we shall see.

HENRY (*moving to Sally*) What's up, Sally?

SALLY (*rising; with an effort*) Nothing.

HENRY. Here—try my shoulder—it's just the right height, I think.

SALLY (*smiling*) Dear Henry.

(GREEN *enters up* L)

GREEN (*crossing to* RC) Pardon me, sir.

HENRY. Forgotten something?

GREEN. I'll say. Been on me mind the past hour. Couldn't think what it was. I was just lowering the third pint when—stone the crows—I remembered. (*He moves up* RC, *peers into the upstage bench and pulls Bradley up by the ear*) Hey, wake up! Rise and shine! Case over—time to go home.

BRADLEY *starts into life as—*

the CURTAIN *falls*

FURNITURE AND PROPERTY LIST

ACT I

SCENE 1

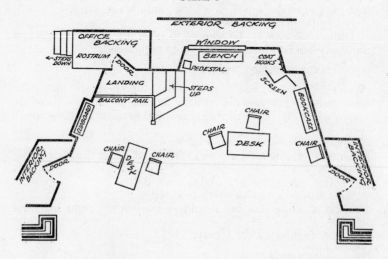

On stage: Desk (R) *On it:* typewriter, pile of old briefs, books, ashtray, matches, notepad, pencil, inkstand, clutter of old papers

Desk chair (R)

3 upright chairs

Desk (LC) *On it:* telephone, telephone pad, inkstand, pen, pencils, blotter, ruler, paper clips, typing paper, desk diary, documents, new briefs, files, small vase of flowers, cigarettes, matches, ashtray

Desk chair (LC)

Bench (up C)

Pedestal (up RC) *On it:* vase

Cupboard (R)

Bookshelves (L) *In them:* law books

3-fold screen

Picture of Grimes in uniform

On floor C: 2 briefs

Coat hooks (up L)

Off stage: Ledgers, fee-book, law books (ALEC)
　　　　　 Newspaper (SALLY)
　　　　　 File (ALEC)
　　　　　 Wig, gown, bands (GRIMES)
　　　　　 Blue bag. *In it:* wig and gown (ROGER)

Personal: SALLY: hat, handbag
　　　　　 ALEC: watch, bag of toffees
　　　　　 MRS THURSBY: handbag
　　　　　 GRIMES: hat

SCENE 2

Strike: Grimes' hat
　　　　 Newspaper
　　　　 Typewriter
　　　　 Books from desk R

Set: *On desk* R: Biggs and Pieman documents
　　　 On desk LC: Fisher and Millet documents
　　　 On coat hooks: Sally's hat and coat

Off stage: Brief (GRIMES)
　　　　　 Brief (ALEC)

Personal: JOY: handbag

ACT II

Set: *On desk* R: brief
　　　 On desk LC: brief, documents
　　　 In desk drawer LC: Sally's handbag
　　　 On hooks: Sally's hat and coat

Off stage: File of papers (SALLY)
　　　　　 Brief (ALEC)

Personal: BRADLEY: comic
　　　　　 GREEN: testimonial, indictment, wallet with 2 postal receipts
　　　　　 JOY: engagement ring, handbag

ROGER: case with cigarettes, lighter, coins
MRS NEWENT: handbag

ACT III

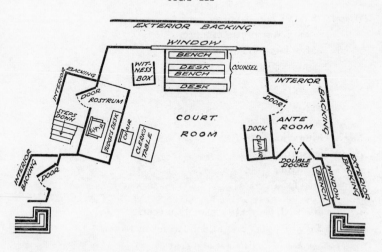

On stage: Bench (down L in corridor)
      Judge's bench. *On it:* pen, pencil, papers, reference books
      Judge's chair
      Clerk's table. *On it:* pen, pencils, inkwell, Bible, card, sealed
          envelope containing discretion statement, various papers
          and reference books
      Clerk's chair
      Witness-box
      Barristers' benches. *On them:* papers, files, reference books
      Dock. *In it:* chair

Off stage: File of papers. *In it:* posting receipts (ROGER)
      Brief (GRIMES)

Personal: ROGER: mirror, watch, handkerchief
      MRS THURSBY: handbag
      BRADLEY: comic
      ALEC: bag of toffees
      JUDGE: watch
      GRIMES: wallet. *In it:* notes

LIGHTING PLOT

Practical fittings required: none

ACT I, SCENE 1. Interior. An office. Morning
    THE MAIN ACTING AREAS are C, and around desks R and LC
    THE APPARENT SOURCE OF LIGHT is a window back C
To open: Effect of daylight
No cues

ACT I, SCENE 2. Morning
To open: Effect of daylight
No cues

ACT II. Morning
To open: Effect of daylight
No cues

ACT III. Interior. A corridor and court-room
    THE MAIN ACTING AREAS are in the corridor down stage; at the
        Judge's bench R, at Counsel's benches up C, at the witness-box
        up RC and at the dock R
    THE APPARENT SOURCE OF LIGHT is a presumed skylight
To open: The stage is in darkness

Cue 1	At the rise of the CURTAIN	(Page 48)
	Bring up lights to cover corridor leaving court-room in dark-ness	
Cue 2	HENRY, SALLY and ALEC exit	(Page 53)
	Dim all lights to BLACK-OUT	
Cue 2a	When ready in court-room	(Page 53)
	Bring up lights on court-room	
Cue 3	CLERK: ". . . at the bar."	(Page 55)
	Dim all lights to BLACK-OUT	
Cue 3a	When ready in court-room	(Page 55)
	Bring up lights on court-room	
Cue 4	GREEN: ". . . speak during lunch."	(Page 58)
	Dim all lights to BLACK-OUT	
Cue 4a	When court-room empty	(Page 58)
	Bring up lights on corridor	
Cue 5	MRS THURSBY: ". . . him the tale?"	(Page 60)
	Dim all lights to BLACK-OUT	
Cue 5a	When ready in court-room	(Page 60)
	Bring up lights on court-room	

EFFECTS PLOT

ACT I

SCENE 1

Cue 1	ALEC: "Conference, two seven." *Telephone rings*	(Page 1)
Cue 2	ALEC: "I'm busy." *Telephone stops ringing*	(Page 1)
Cue 3	SALLY exits *Telephone rings*	(Page 2)
Cue 4	MRS THURSBY: ". . . have heard us." *Telephone stops ringing*	(Page 3)
Cue 5	ROGER: "Actually . . ." *Telephone rings*	(Page 8)

SCENE 2

| Cue 6 | ROGER sits R of desk LC *Telephone rings* | (Page 22) |

ACT II

| Cue 7 | MRS THURSBY: "—I knew it." *Sound of taxi horn* | (Page 44) |

ACT III

| Cue 8 | ROGER: "Thanks very much." *3 loud knocks R* | (Page 61) |